The Radio & Television Commercial

Second Edition

ALBERT C. BOOK
Professor of Journalism
University of Nebraska

NORMAN D. CARY
Senior Associate Professor of Mass Media
Bucks County Community College

STANLEY I. TANNENBAUM
President
Bentley, Barnes & Lynn Advertising, Inc.
Visiting Professor
Northwestern University

CRAIN
BOOKS

740 Rush Street
Chicago, Illinois 60611

Published by Crain Books
A Division of Crain Communications Inc.
740 Rush Street
Chicago, Illinois 60611

86 85 84 10 9 8 7 6 5 4 3 2 1

ISBN 0-87251-095-6

Library of Congress Catalog Card No. 84-45231

Printed in the United States of America

Cover design: Dick Travis

Contents

Preface

Like most businesses, advertising combines science and fact with art and creativity. Science and fact can be absorbed, reflected on, and utilized, while art and creativity can be encouraged, guided, and developed. Our primary purpose in this book is to help develop the art of creating effective radio and television advertising.

In this book, we hope to reach and direct the individual who may be preparing for a career in advertising, marketing, or associated areas in industry. To do this, we analyze the techniques of current radio and television commercial formats and offer practical guides toward producing and judging well-designed sales messages in these media.

Millions of dollars of advertisers' money are wasted each year because commercials are carelessly designed, poorly written, and amateurishly produced. This book, perhaps serving as a background for a copywriter, producer, art director, agency account executive, or advertising manager, can help reduce the number of such failures.

Some day in the future, you may help create commercials while working for an ad agency, or you may sit in judgment on them as a client. Right now, we look at you as a person with ideas. We hope the ideas will be fresh and original. With a developed sense of form and craftsmanship, you can incorporate these ideas into commercials that will be noticed and acted on.

A creator of radio and television commercials must answer to his own conscience in matters of honesty, taste, and discretion. How he accepts this responsibility is vital to his success as an advertising practitioner and is just as vital to his sense of personal integrity.

A.C.B.
N.C.
S.T.

Section One:
Broadcast Advertising

Creating The Commercial 1

Selling is as old as man's recorded history. Ancient businessmen of Ephesus and Pompeii carved sales messages in stone. Early bazaars displayed goods, and merchants extolled their products with words and gestures. Street vendors in old England developed special cries and songs for their cakes or fruit or flowers. Long before most people could even read or write, inns and taverns advertised themselves with signs that indicated their commercial purposes. Barber poles and pawn-broker symbols still exist to serve as instantly recognizable reminders of the specific services offered to the public.

Because of the late development of printing and the slow increase in literacy, advertising did not appear in print until the 18th century. Magazines, with their eventual development of high-quality color reproduction, greatly aided the beginnings of mass marketing in the print media. With the advent of radio, using sound and music, and television, adding sight and motion, advertisers could take full advantage of mass communications for the purpose of sales persuasion.

Consumer Criticism

However, along with the opportunity to appeal to potential consumers in a new and powerful way, radio and television brought with them certain disadvantages. The first is higher cost—and therefore greater risk. The second is based on the fundamentally different ways that prospects respond to broadcast and print. A newspaper or magazine ad can be totally ignored, quickly scanned, or thoroughly read. The time the reader devotes to each message depends on the interest aroused and sustained by the ad itself. Television and radio commercials interrupt programing content as a print advertisement interrupts the editorial content of a magazine or newspaper. However, audio and audio/visual commercials are more abrupt, more obtrusive, more jarring. This is because they momentarily displace everything else in the medium. They force themselves on the viewer's or listener's consciousness. And they must run out their time span before the audience can return its attention to other contents of the medium.

Of course, the audience can stop watching television or listening to the radio, just as it can stop reading a newspaper or magazine. But even on this point, the broadcast media are significantly less avoidable than the print media. If the viewer looks away from the TV screen or even steps out of the room, he still may be able to hear the audio portion. And the same is true of radio. If you want to stop reading a print ad, you just close your eyes, turn the page, or direct your attention elsewhere. If you want to stop listening to a broadcast commercial, however, and you don't own a remote control device, you must rise from your chair and get out of hearing range, turn off the receiver, or switch channels.

The results are twofold. First, in radio and TV, the audience is more or less "captive." And this is a distinct advantage. Second, however, the commercial interruption may cause impatience or irritation. Forced to choose between seeing and/or hearing, on the one hand, and turning off the medium, on the other, the prospect can be more easily attracted *and* more easily offended. No wonder, then, that the public's responses to radio and television commercials are more vocal and more varied than they are to print advertisements.

While most listeners and viewers accept the fact that commercials are the price they must pay for "free" television and radio programing, many express negative opinions of broadcast ads. According to a study by Elmo Roper and Associates, although the public's attitude toward TV commercials in particular is more favorable than hostile, the number of people who actively dislike them is substantial.

Commercial Failure

Yet, despite the criticism, radio and television have grown steadily as advertising media. In fact, many spots that have been publicly decried as irritating and obtrusive have succeeded where success counts most—not in winning prizes or in garnering praise for being responsive to consumer criticism, but in selling products. Love-hate relationships aside, the objective of a commercial is to get the prospect to stop, look, listen—

1

and act. And radio and TV spots must be judged, at least by the advertisers who pay for them, on the basis of that criterion alone.

In that context, both radio and television are extremely effective. Television combines sight, color, voices, music, movement, sound, and visual effects. For its part, radio offers an involving mixture of voice, music, sound effects, and, importantly, unbridled use of the imagination.

However, although the effectiveness of these media has been amply demonstrated, commercials do not always succeed. In fact, the question must be asked why so many commercials do not attract and intrigue the listener or viewer and end up either ignored or forgotten. That is, why do they fail to sell? Of course, there are many answers to this question, but three keep recurring in research. First, many copywriters take for granted that the name of the product or service will be remembered, even though experts have insisted that almost two-thirds of all commercials do not register the name. Second, the construction of many commercials is haphazard to the point of weakness. And third, many TV and radio spots are imitative, even trite. These practices show a costly disregard for the viewer or listener. They insult his taste and intelligence. And they therefore arouse resentment or generate apathy.

About 50,000 TV commercials are produced in the United States each year. The number of radio commercials is all but incalculable. Since TV viewing and radio listening norms vary, it is difficult to estimate how many of these commercials are actually seen and heard. But it has been suggested that a young adult might hear 2,500 radio spots and view about 1,000 TV spots each month. For the reasons given above, only a handful of these can be considered outstanding selling vehicles. Fewer win awards.

Evidence of the combined skills of creative craftsmen in radio and television advertising can be found among the award winners of a number of annual competitions, both regional and national. The winners of the gold statuette Clio awards (presented at the American Television and Radio Commercials Festival) enter the highest chamber of the pantheon. Yet, as many advertising professionals claim, awards aren't everything. Much of the judging, they say, concentrates on innovative techniques and/or entertaining (i.e., humorous) approaches, rather than on sales effectiveness. This point is well taken. Some commercials, although award winners in competition, have been abject failures in producing sales. Other commercials, not even considered for an award, have led to dramatic upswings in sales curves.

The Need for Creativity

Obviously, the key ingredient in any successful commercial is creativity. But the word is so often used and misused that it is important to determine exactly what it means in order to find out how it applies to advertising.

The distinguished writer John Steinbeck wrote in *East of Eden* (Viking Press, 1952): "Our species is the only creative species, and it has only one creative instrument: the individual mind and spirit of man. Nothing was ever created by two men. There are no good collaborations, whether in music, in art, in poetry, in mathematics, in philosophy. Once the miracle of creation has taken place, the group can develop it, but the group never invents anything."

Taken in its purest sense, this is true. Ideas do begin "in the lonely mind of a man." And, in any commercial, the *idea* is the spark that, fanned into flame by keen craftsmanship, lifts the commercial above mediocrity and achieves something distinctive, memorable, and effective. Without a strong central idea a commercial is likely to be dull, prosaic, imitative—and ineffective.

How do ideas begin to take form? Psychologists from William James on have explored the question. Dr. Gary Steiner narrows the search to commercials in *The People Look at Television* (Knopf, 1963). "Every creative idea," he says, "is initially a departure from present ways of doing things." Writers depart from an accepted, workable base because times change, attitudes change, taste and fashions change. And these things change all the more quickly in a society that has a high degree of mobility and a vast quantity of communications. Each change brings with it a new problem or set of problems. So, in the business of marketing and selling, in the use of advertising, new solutions must be found to new problems. And this demands thinking in new ways and combinations.

Dr. Steiner defines creativity as "the ability to produce and implement new and better solutions to any kind of a problem—to the writing of the copy, to the problem of deciding where and when to advertise, to the problem of how to organize a company." A copywriter's ability is always challenged to "produce and implement new and better solutions"—especially when he or she is pressured by time, budget, and competitive limitations.

While poets create to enlighten and composers to entertain, advertising writers create to change minds and alter buying decisions. This function of creativity should be kept constantly in mind. William Bernbach, the late chairman and cofounder of Doyle Dane Bernbach, summed it up when he reported on the planning of an important campaign: "We had neither the time nor the money to impress our message through sheer weight and repetition. We had to call in our ally—creativity. We had to startle people into an immediate awareness of our advantages in such a way that they would never forget it."

Getting Started

Wanted: a selling campaign! A unique slogan, memorable music, and a dazzling combination of words and pictures—all designed to persuade consumers to buy your product. How does it happen? How is that attention-getting and purchase-inducing radio or television commercial actually created?

The writing of a commercial is usually done by one or two members of the agency creative department. But it often takes 10, 20, or even more advertiser and agency people to get the copywriter and artist to the point where they have enough information to write an effective commercial. In fact, the writing of a radio or TV spot is the last step in a long creative process that requires the participation of many specialists and can consume a great amount of time.

At the advertising agency, the creative process starts with the formation of an account group made up of executives from the account management, creative, media, and research departments. The members of the account group are specialists with years of experience in communicating with the consumer. For the advertiser, the process begins with the establishment of a product group, whose area of expertise is the development and marketing of products. Ordinarily, the advertiser product group is made up of a marketing director, a product manager, a product research/development manager, and a marketing research director. The agency account group and the advertiser product group work closely together. Their common goal is to develop an advertising strategy that will lead to the creation of advertising that will solve the product's marketing problem.

The "assignment"—the request from the client for advertising work by the agency—can come in many forms. If the product is new, the assignment will contain marketing objectives, which may be stated in terms of consumer acceptance, dollar sales, share of market, and/or product trial. If the product has been on the market, the assignment may contain revisions of the original objectives or new objectives stated in terms of specific marketing problems.

For example, research may show that, although consumers like the product, they believe it isn't worth the price. Or consumers may consider the product's taste, performance, or durability to be inferior to that of the competition. Or perhaps the product has been hit by a competitive attack on TV that has made people switch brands only because they have been entertained by the competitor's advertising. Whatever the problem, it must be found, analyzed, and defined, usually by the product group. The assignment of solving the problem is then given by the product manager to the agency account manager. In turn, the account manager calls a meeting of the account group, at which the marketing problem is thoroughly discussed and specific tasks are assigned.

Responsibilities

The account manager has the major responsibility for everything the agency does for the client, from advertising strategy to actual commercials. He serves as a liaison between the client and every department within the agency. He provides information from the client to these departments. And he keeps the client abreast of the agency's progress. Because he must make sure that advertiser and agency understand each other, he must listen attentively and communicate clearly. And because he is in charge, he must organize the project carefully and efficiently.

The creative director, or the assigned copywriter/artist team, is responsible for turning out the finished product. His first task is to find out everything there is to know about the product, the consumer, and the competition. The more questions he asks, the better. Questions lead to hunches. Hunches lead to hypotheses. And hypotheses eventually lead to strategies, which lead to finished radio and television commercials. The creative director must work closely with agency and client research people. He must talk to consumers, retailers, and product distributors. Then, after he has acquired the information he needs, he must live and think the product, the consumer, and the competition 24 hours a day, seven days a week.

The research representative of the account group is responsible for gathering secondary and organizing primary research about the product, the consumer, and the competition. He should work closely with the creative people assigned to the group to help satisfy their need for information. That information will consist of data supplied by the research people in the product group and by the agency research department's own studies.

The media person in the group is assigned the job of finding out what competition is doing in the various media. How much are they spending? Where? Why? Who is their target market? Are they spending their media money effectively? Is there anything to be learned about the potential customer from his media habits? Do his media preferences indicate that one medium would work better than others?

The client product group should continue to provide the agency with as much information as possible and to communicate its hunches about the best way to sell the product. Members of the group should be available to answer questions, discuss new thoughts, and generally act as both a catalyst and a sounding board for strategies and ideas throughout the entire course of the project.

Developing the Strategy

The creative process is much like solving a puzzle. And the puzzle is complicated. Who is the person most likely to buy your product? How is he influenced by the advertising for competitive products? What is your basic promise to the consumer? Is it strong enough to win customers away from competition? How do you support the promise so that the prospect will believe it? Solving the puzzle—developing the creative or marketing strategy—can take weeks or months. You sometimes resort to brainstorming or other idea-generating techniques. Often, you call in outside experts. You attend many formal meetings and participate in scores of informal discussions. You use research to help you test your hunches and hypotheses.

One of the most commonly used research methods at this stage in the process is the product concept test. Here, numerous product concepts, sales propositions, are tested with representative samples of the target market. They are simply worded "promises" to consumers indicating what the product can or will do for them. The creative person in the account group writes the various propositions to be tested. These concepts are not phrased as advertising statements. In fact, the less they sound like advertising jargon, the more useful they are.

The creative director (or the creative team) works on developing the "personality" of the product. He also helps decide which kind of testing will be needed to determine which type of commercial will produce the desired personality. He should be involved in creating and selecting the best "reason why," or supporting, statements that will make the selling idea believable. And he should participate in choosing the product's brand name, designing the package, writing the label copy, and determining the price—all the elements that help create the product's personality and help support the selling idea.

When all the answers are in, the account group writes a creative or advertising strategy statement (see Exhibits 1-1 and 1-2). This statement should be a one-page document that
1. Describes the product in real and perceived terms
2. Defines the target customer
3. Defines the competition and what it is saying to the target customer
4. States the one *competitive* benefit that the product offers the target customer
5. States the support for that benefit
6. Describes the tone of the advertising that will create the personality of the product

While the strategy statement should be restricted to one page, every section of the statement must be accompanied by a rationale that explains or proves the point being made. The rationale usually contains a definitive analysis of the product, including both product facts and consumer perceptions. The statement should show why the target consumer was chosen over other alternatives. And it should indicate how the competitive promise that will be made to the consumer will be supported and made acceptable and believable. One section of the statement should define the objectives of the advertising (what it is expected to accomplish) and the means by which these objectives will be fulfilled (what media will be used to expose the advertising).

Before any advertising is written, the creative or advertising strategy statement must be approved by agency management, including agency principals and, very often, a strategy review committee that consists of the top marketing, media, research, and creative people in the agency. After this approval, the strategy must be approved by the client product group and, in most cases, by the top management of the client company.

Finding the Commercial Idea

After the strategy statement has been approved, the creative director is in charge. It's his or her responsibility to create a commercial that will catch fire with the consumer—a commercial that will be unique, memorable, and successful. So he sets out to deliver the consumer promise, the selling idea, with an unforgettable slogan, a catchy jingle, or a hilarious series of vignettes that will be talked about at coffee klatches and honored at the American Radio and Television Commercial Festival. And, in all this, he must adhere strictly to the guidelines expressed or implied in the strategy statement.

This sounds easy enough. But how does it happen? The answer is: very slowly and sometimes very painfully. After agency and advertiser approval, the creative director gives the assignment to teams of copywriters and art directors. As the names suggest, the copywriter is responsible for the words and the art director for the pictures and graphics. In practice, however, with talented teams of writers and artists, it is more accurate to say that both are responsible for the "idea" of the commercial. The idea may come from a drawing or a set of words, or both, and it may have been created by either one of the creative team members.

How long does it take to develop the commercial idea? Some creative teams can come up with 30 or 40 ideas in a day. Other teams may develop only one idea in a week. The members of each team can work separately or together. If they decide to split up, they may periodically get together with each other or even with other teams to discuss their ideas. The purpose of such meetings is to try out these ideas on other people. The result is the development of a number of possible ideas that have gone through a series of alterations, adaptations, and refinements.

This period of gestation is also a narrowing-down process. Eventually, inappropriate or unworkable ideas are eliminated, and all the potentially good ideas are committed to paper, either in rough storyboard form or in a two- or three-sentence paragraph. Usually, if the idea is very good, you will be able to communicate it in one sentence or with a storyboard that consists of a couple of simply drawn sketches and a few words of copy.

The commercial ideas are then presented by the copywriter and art director teams to the creative director. At this point, ideas that have merit are critiqued, and assignments are given to change or develop them. Often, more meetings are held for the purpose of discussing the modifications of the original ideas or to consider ideas that may have arisen in the meantime.

Choosing the Right Idea

The first or second round of creative exploration may have produced 20 or 30 rough ideas worth considering. The final refinement stage may have reduced the list of viable ideas to five or six. Now it is up to the creative director to make a selection. The decision is by no means easy. The director has to decide which of the commercials submitted by the various creative teams will be recommended to agency and client management and, if approved, eventually produced.

The creative director is usually advised by other members of the account group. Often, the research person tests the selected commercial ideas, even though they are only in preliminary stages of production. This research tries to ascertain whether the points in the creative strategy statement have been made: if the commercial attracts attention, if it appeals to the right consumer, and if it says the right thing—and says it persuasively.

Once the agency approves a commercial, it must be presented to the client, including the product group and, more often than not, top management. The recommended commercial is usually presented by the copywriter and artist who created it because they know the idea better than anyone else. The finished storyboard or radio script is usually presented with a rationale that tells what the commercial is intended to accomplish, how it will accomplish it, and why, based on research results, it can be expected to accomplish it.

The Creative Process Is the Rule

What has been described above is the way the creative process ordinarily works in a large advertising agency. But even a small agency or a one-man agency should follow a step-by-step method because it can lead to more effective advertising. However, some agencies may shortcut the process under special circumstances. For example, it is sometimes impractical to take the time and trouble to write a complete strategy statement for a product that the agency is soliciting in a new business presentation; all the marketing data may not be available. And it is not always necessary to devote a large amount of time to a successful brand with a minor marketing problem. In such cases, agency and advertiser may choose to update the existing strategy. On the other hand, in the marketing development of a new product, an agency and client may take even more time, use even more people's expertise, and apply the creative process to such areas as product ingredients, quality, design, and performance.

Exhibit 1-1. Strategy Statement: Kwik 'n Kool

PRODUCT: Kwik 'n Kool, distributed by Dunsmore Beverage Co., is a powdered fruit drink. Its granules dissolve in hot or cold water. It contains an artificial sweetener and imitation fruit flavor. There are five Kwik 'n Kool flavors: orange, strawberry, lime, lemon, and Oahu (a combination citrus and pineapple). The tastes closely approximate those of natural fruit juices. But Kwik 'n Kool has no appreciable health benefit.

Each flavor comes packed in a three- by five-inch flat aluminum foil envelope sealed all around. The name "Kwik 'n Kool" is printed in cursive across the face of the front of the package. A picture of the fruit flavor and its name appear on the lower part of the front. Directions for mixing are printed on the back of the package. Each package costs 49¢, 2 cents less than its nearest competitor.

One package makes two quarts. All five flavors can be used together as punch or as the main ingredient of a party punch. Children can easily mix and make Kwik 'n Kool.

Presently, consumers perceive the product as a "cheap" but nondescript alternative to its costlier and more well-positioned competitors.

CONSUMER: Children 5 to 15 years old account for 90% of consumption. Adult use amounts to 3% and children in the 16-21 age bracket consume 7%. The target market is 8-12 year olds in order to hit the center of the existing market and to establish a uniformly directed advertising campaign.

COMPETITION: Kwik 'n Kool has only 15% of the powdered fruit drink market. The competition includes two powdered drinks (Kool-Aid and Hawaiian Punch), three ready-made drinks (Hawaiian Punch, Capri Sun, and Hi-C), fruit juices, and soft drinks. The direct competitors, the two powdered drink makers, target the low and high end of the 5-15-year-old market, respectively. In recent campaigns, Kool-Aid has run slice-of-life TV spots focusing on children's leisure-time activities with only minimal emphasis on the product. Hawaiian Punch has used both radio and television for airing musicals featuring well-known teenage personalities.

COMPETITIVE BENEFIT: Kwik 'n Kool is an easy-to-make, good-tasting, and refreshing summertime drink. However, since the product shares these benefits with competitors, its main competitive difference will be established by its association with children in the designated age group. In addition, although other powdered fruit drinks are equally "quick" and "cool", they have not emphasized these benefits. So advertising should focus on children in the targeted group enjoying both aspects of the product's name.

SUPPORT: These competitive benefits can be stressed by showing children preparing and drinking Kwik 'n Kool while they are "having fun." They could be shown taking the package from a kitchen shelf, mixing powder and water, and drinking the results. These events might take place after "hard" play and before the smiles that indicate satisfaction.

TONE: The advertising should be fast-paced and entertaining. It should establish a clear connection between Kwik 'n Kool and summertime recreation: sports, picnics, vacations. The product should be perceived as the "fun" drink for busy and active children and as indispensable to their frenetically pursued free-time activities.

Exhibit 1-2. Strategy Statement: Gro-Slo

PRODUCT: Gro-Slo, a grass-growth inhibitor, is a chemical compound in pellet form. Each pellet is one and one-quarter inches in diameter and has four small holes (arranged like those in a button). Grass-green in color. Toxic. (Pellets should be kept away from children and pets but will not harm them once it has been applied to grass.) A special applicator need be purchased just once. It can be attached to the standard garden hose for application.

Once the Gro-Slo solution is broadcast, the chemical goes to work on leaf and root. It retards the growth of grass--even crab grass. Because the pellets dissolve in water, rain only helps Gro-Slo reach the roots. One application covers 1,000 square feet of lawn. Three applications from April through September should suffice.

The original purchase will be a package ten by four inches in size. It will contain the plastic attachment (with a built-in screen to hold the pellets against the rush of water) and a plastic bag containing a dozen pellets. A printed set of instructions is included. Subsequent packages of pellets can be bought without the applicator attachment. These packages are 5 x 1½ x 1½ inches in size. The original package will be priced at $14.95. Pellet packages will cost $6.95.

CONSUMER: Gro-Slo will be available nationally, but promotional activity will be concentrated in the Southeast. The product will be sold in independent and chain hardware stores, garden centers, and large discount stores. The traditional market for grass-growth inhibitors has been proprietors of golf courses and athletic fields in warm, humid climates, especially in the Southeast. Gro-Slo is aiming for the general consumer market in this region. Potential buyers are middle-income, homeowning males, 35-60 years old, who are concerned about lawn care but are interested in time-saving methods.

COMPETITION: The lone competitor presently promotes the product almost exclusively to golf course owners and grounds maintenance supervisors at schools and colleges. The product, sold in granular form and packaged in 40-pound bags, is less expensive per square foot of application than Gro-Slo, but it is unavailable in retail outlets. It is broadcast by means of a two-wheeled, manual or a full-size mechanical spreader.

COMPETITIVE BENEFIT: In areas of the country in which growing grass is a problem rather than a solution, Gro-Slo can save homeowners time and money. Three applications annually can reduce grass-cutting time by half.

SUPPORT: The benefit can be made credible and attractive by dramatizing the ease and infrequency of application and the reduction in lawn maintenance time resulting from use.

TONE: Although the message can be presented either humorously or seriously, the commercial as a whole should support an image of integrity for the company and of reliability for the product, including both ingredients and applicator. Therefore, if humor is used, it should not be farcical or silly. It must suggest to the audience that, although both company and product are new, they are dependable.

Developing The Idea 2

Writing radio and TV commercials today is more difficult in some ways and easier in others than it was a generation ago. Fortunately, this apparent paradox has an explanation. Years ago, technology was rudimentary. Most commercials, both network and local, were performed live, and experienced writers, actors, and technicians were not always available. Special effects, including music, were often imitative and unsophisticated. Every non-live element had to be performed, cued, and mixed at the very moment the disc or film was being produced. The processing sometimes took days for radio and months for film.

Today, the state of the art has improved dramatically. Participants in both the creation and production of broadcast commercials are specialists in the field. Audio and video taperecording equipment and procedures are virtually flawless. Multitracks are common. Microphones and mixing and editing equipment have been perfected. In TV, lightweight cameras, instant special effects, and computerized optics are almost universally available. Thus, you have more latitude in creativity and production. You can do much more, and you can do it much better. But this wider choice of talents and techniques also renders decision making far more complicated and therefore far more difficult.

Understand the Obstacles

Two other elements add to the problem of writing persuasive radio and television spots. First, advertising competition has burgeoned as stations and channels have multiplied. It is tougher to gain and hold the audience's attention. Second, the listener and viewer have changed. Because of the growing number of advertising impressions in all media, many people have learned, consciously or unconsciously, to block out unwanted sights and sounds. Loud, repetitive, and simplistic radio and TV spots are considered by some members of the audience to be eye and ear pollutants.

In addition, a number of special problems exist in each medium. People no longer sit in their living rooms quietly and more or less passively listening to the radio as they did in pretelevision days. They have radios in just about every room in the house. And they are often doing something other than just listening. A housewife may be preparing dinner, ironing, trying to get the kids off to school, or perhaps just chatting with a neighbor. A teenager may be doing his homework, making a snack, or talking on the telephone. In both cases, the listener is unlikely to be riveted to the radio. Furthermore, your commercial may come on as a driver weaves through traffic, a vacationist suns on the beach, a patient waits in a dentist's office, a farmer feeds his cattle, a man shaves, or a couple parks on the side of the road. Unlike your TV audience, your radio audience might be anywhere, and its attention is very likely to be divided.

Finally, the person doing the housework might be a man rather than a woman. And the driver threading through rush-hour traffic might be a woman rather than a man. The result is that you compete not only with other advertisers and their products, but with other activities—some of them totally distracting. And your target audience may not be where you think it is. It may not even be *who* you think it is.

Of course, radio advertising still retains its inherent selling powers. And, for this reason, most copywriters happily accept the challenge of both breaking through the competitive clutter and finding the right listener. In fact, the discipline of writing radio commercials under difficult conditions is generally regarded as exceptionally good training. According to Warren Pfaff, former senior vice president of J. Walter Thompson: "If you want to be a good writer, think about radio first. Radio's the little box without eyes, and it doesn't give you an art director to lean on; it doesn't give you any socko picture to bail you out. You're all alone with the listener, and somehow you've got to hit him between the eyes even when his eyes are closed. Once you've learned to do that, you've just got to be a better writer. In any medium."

The need for "breakthrough" writing is just as great in television as it is in radio—perhaps even greater. The double hit of sound and picture can make TV commercials more intrusive and potentially much more annoying than radio. The sheer number of commercials viewers are exposed to is mind-boggling. According to researcher A. C. Nielsen, the average household spends about seven hours a day either watching TV or listening to it, or both. This means that the viewer may see as many as 100 to 150 commercials a day. And they come in clusters of six or eight or ten at a time, and in varying lengths of 10, 15, 30, and 60 seconds, all fighting for a share of the public's mind. The viewer would have to be a computer to identify, recognize, or remember them. And he would have to be fitted with a presently unavailable program to be able to distinguish one from the other.

What's more, after years and years of television commercial bombardment, the audience has become somewhat cynical. Not only is it difficult to penetrate the clutter, but TV viewers have set up barriers of disbelief, which all TV writers must consider. It's getting so that viewers have come to distrust the truth. In addition, because of the look-alike nature of most commercials, brand name recognition among major advertisers is lower than it ever was, despite the millions of dollars spent on getting consumers just to recognize a product's name.

Use Your Research

Before you even think of putting pencil to paper, you must study all the facts given to you by agency and client researchers. Examine this data in relation to the following areas of concern:

1. *Know your customers and prospects.* Who buys your kind of product? Who uses your services? Where? How often? Why? Put yourself in your customer's shoes. Get to know what need might trigger a desire for your product. Is the need emotional? Is the desire practical? Again, ask many questions in your consumer research.

2. *Know your product (or service).* Inside and out. What is it? How is it made? What needs does it satisfy? How? What makes it better than the competition? Does it contain any special ingredients? Is it manufactured in an unusual way? Competent research should elicit dozens of such questions. Be sure to get specific answers to all of them.

3. *Know your competition.* What other products or services similar to yours are available? How are they made? What features are better or worse than those of your product? How? Why? Are they virtually similar, like many cigarettes, beer, and gasolines? Your market and advertising research should explore their selling themes and performance claims. Does competition have a genuine, demonstrable advantage, or has it merely preempted a shared performance characteristic?

When you are satisfied that you know who your customers are, what needs your product satisfies, and how your product compares with competition, you may

feel somewhat overwhelmed. But you must have these facts in order to create a sound marketing plan and a clear-cut creative strategy.

Think, Then Write

The genesis of an idea can be purely inspirational and can occur any time after you have absorbed the basic creative strategy. But don't count on it. An enormous amount of concentrated thought can go into the development of a selling idea. Facts fed into your consciousness boil and turn. They are even affected by your subconscious. An idea for a bread commercial came to David Ogilvy and awoke him out of a sound sleep. He wrote it down and used it the next day to create an appealing TV spot. Of course, much conscious thought had already gone into solving the problem. It is a popular belief that there are no new ideas, only refreshing combinations of old ones, so don't overlook possible combinations or extensions in your thinking.

Once you have some ideas on paper, choose a friend or co-worker and try out your copy approaches. A fresh mind can often spot a weakness that you have failed to see. Better yet, by verbalizing your approach, you may find that you can more readily select and modify an idea by seeing it in a new light or at a unique angle.

Even experienced pros sometimes run into a dry spell. There are ways to get your thoughts going again if you seem to be stuck temporarily. These vary with individuals. Some sleep on the problem. Some take up another chore and return to the problem with fresh perspective. Others flail away at typewriter and drawing pad and put down dozens of thoughts, almost any thoughts, wild or tame, hopeful that one may lead to the selling idea.

Here is one helpful suggestion. Choose a friend and write him a letter (one you probably won't send). Make it sincere, persuasive, and, because he is your good friend, personal. Try to convince him of your product's advantages. Loosen your writing style, be your real self, communicate on a one-to-one basis. Such a relationship, not so incidentally, is the basis of radio and TV selling: Although your audience may number in the millions, you direct your appeal to one person at a time. As your letter develops, you may discover yourself writing about the product in a different, new way. A gem of an idea may strike you and, figuratively, leap off the page.

Test & Revise

When you feel confident that you have a solid, worthwhile selling idea, compare it with the selling themes of your competitors. Be as objective as you can. Try it out on someone whose opinion you value. Check it against your marketing and advertising objectives. (See Exhibits 2-1 and 2-2.) If it doesn't quite fit, work with variations of the idea. Move words around. Substitute. But always cast it in terms of your prospect's self-interest.

Words and sounds (and, for television, any possible visual treatment) are your basic materials, but the connotations and denotations of words are your allies. Just as outstanding chefs can give a special taste to a run-of-the-menu recipe, so too can an imaginative creator of TV or radio spots bring uniqueness to a selling theme. Words can shock, soothe, stimulate, agitate (even as these words evoke a response in you). Active words, words with vitality, can give your selling theme life and vigor. Be sure that they communicate precisely and truthfully. Make them move your prospect to attention, agreement, acceptance, and action.

If your product's name can become part of the selling idea, you are closer to success. Old Milwaukee beer takes advantage of the fact that it is named for "the city that means beer." The makers of L'eggs stockings and pantyhose have combined a sophisticated mixture of name, product use, and an easily recognizable package. McDonald's uses the first syllable in its name for various products, such as Eggs McMuffin and Chicken McNuggets. And 7UP positioned itself as unique by calling itself the "Uncola."

Say It All—Simply

With a strong selling idea within a memorable theme or phrase, you are ready to give it persuasive shape as a radio or television commercial. An obvious next question involves what format the commercial will follow. However, while you may have had some thoughts about format, structure, and style during the development process, it is dangerous to consider such elements before you determine the selling idea. Putting the commercial cart before the motivating horse often obstructs the way and impedes progress toward a fresh, new approach.

Above all, keep your selling idea easy to understand. Your theme or phrase may be as short as the successful "Coke is it!" It may be as extended as the early Clairol line: "Does she or doesn't she? Only her hairdresser knows for sure."

In the cola example, Coca-Cola was fighting to enhance and extend its share of the market and reaffirming its preeminence, originality, and "firstness" in the field. By saying that Coke is "it"—that is, the *real* cola—Coca-Cola seems to be inviting the prospect to infer that other colas are imitative and less authentic.

In the Clairol case, hair coloring was treated as a contemporary, natural-looking, entirely acceptable thing to do in a decade when it still was considered rather bold. Attractive young mothers were shown informally with their attractive young children. A female listener/viewer could conclude from the ads that she would neither look unnatural nor be subject to the raised eyebrow or a fall from social acceptance. Here, the visual treatment reinforced the words. This one brand helped establish an entire market and paved the way for the many types and brands of hair coloring now taken for granted.

Include your product's name in the selling theme. In an effective cat food spot, cats ask for Meow cat food by name. In another spot, the phrase "Bounty—the quicker picker-upper" gets both name and claims into its short selling line. Never forget that competition is tough and apt to get tougher. You must get listeners and viewers to recall the product name, remember what the product does, and know how it performs.

Select a Format

As your commercial unfolds, the sales message should come through clearly. The appropriate format should be there to support it, move it along, and give it a framework. If you find the format draws attention to itself and obscures the product name, you're probably working with the wrong format.

With an effective sales theme in a compatible format, your commercial stands a better chance of attracting attention, involving the prospective customer emotionally and logically, developing a desire to try the product, and leading him to buy it.

In creating and crafting, you are fortunate in that you have easy access to radio and television. By attentive listening and watching, you can become more aware of different selling ideas and how they are presented. As you watch and listen, you should ask a number of questions—and answer them. Are the spots direct and clear? Are they obscure? Do they state benefits? Imply? Do they appeal to emotion or logic?

Questions such as these should be asked when you study the examples of radio and television commercials in Chapters 6 and 9. Note the variety of formats and how the selling ideas are used within them. Be alert to their simplicity, clarity, and strong name identification.

Choose an Appeal

The format alone can't make a commercial successful. Your TV or radio spot must have a logical or emotional appeal. If the format can be considered the vehicle, then the appeal can be thought of as the fuel—the energy that makes your vehicle go where you want it to go and do what you want it to do.

If your product outperforms the competition, there must be a reason. The sheer weight or logic of fact might persuade a prospect. If your product has parity of performance with the competition, you must search for the one advantage or difference that can be translated into a dramatic sensory or emotional appeal. Health, safety, home, sex, love, and sentiment are strong personal concerns, and ads for products with benefits in these areas should exploit their psychological advantage.

Concern for status—whether personal, family, or group—evolves from the need for esteem, one of the strongest bases for an emotional appeal. Almost everyone wants to be appreciated, whether by looking better or feeling better. Of course, your research (on custo-

Exhibit 2-1. Marketing Objectives: Xerox

MARKETING:

To expand the use of Xerox machines to central reproduction centers characterized by high-volume duplicating. To compete in this market, a new high-speed machine with automatic collating capability was developed.

ADVERTISING:

To establish awareness of the new copier. To communicate that Xerox is an advanced technology company, a good corporate citizen, and a company whose advertising is distinctive and memorable.

Advertiser: Xerox Corp.

Agency: Needham, Harper & Steers, Inc.

Product: Xerox 9200 Duplicating System

Title: "Monks"

Format: Problem-solution

Length: 60 seconds

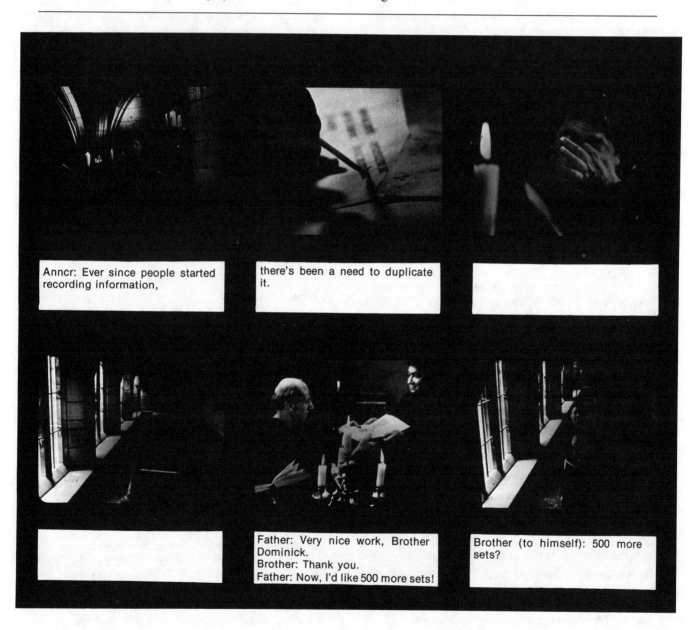

Anncr: Ever since people started recording information,

there's been a need to duplicate it.

Father: Very nice work, Brother Dominick.
Brother: Thank you.
Father: Now, I'd like 500 more sets!

Brother (to himself): 500 more sets?

Stephens: Brother Dominick, what can I do for you?

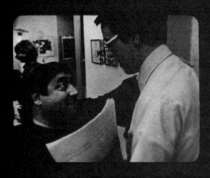

Brother: Could you do a big job for me?

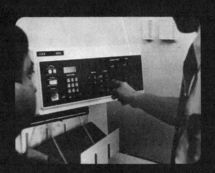

Announcer, V.O.: Xerox has developed an amazing machine that's unlike anything we've ever made. The Xerox 9200 Duplicating

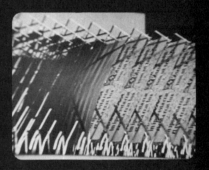

System. It automatically feeds and cycles originals . . . Has a computerized programmer that coordinates the entire system.

Can duplicate, reduce and assemble a virtually limitless number of complete sets . . .

Brother: Here are your sets, Father.
Father: What?
Bro.: The 500 sets you asked for.

Father: It's a miracle!

Exhibit 2-2. Marketing Objectives: Alpo

MARKETING:

From the beginning, Alpo has been positioned as a high-quality, all-meat dog food—a "natural" favorite of all types of dogs. The objective of this campaign is to attract new users and maintain present users.

ADVERTISING:

To convince dog food customers, primarily those using canned dog food, that Alpo is good for dogs for two reasons. First, it has a high level of beef and meat by-products. And second, Alpo is a complete and balanced diet.

Advertiser: Allen Products Co., Inc.

Agency: Weightman, Inc.

Product: Alpo dog food

Title: "ALPO Time"

Format: Testimonial

Length: 60 seconds

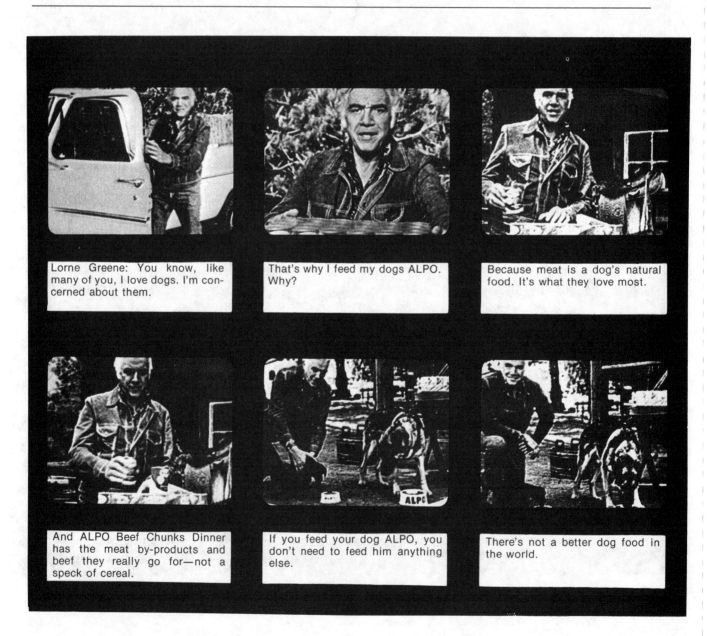

Lorne Greene: You know, like many of you, I love dogs. I'm concerned about them.

That's why I feed my dogs ALPO. Why?

Because meat is a dog's natural food. It's what they love most.

And ALPO Beef Chunks Dinner has the meat by-products and beef they really go for—not a speck of cereal.

If you feed your dog ALPO, you don't need to feed him anything else.

There's not a better dog food in the world.

Lorne Greene: You want to see something? Watch this.

C'mon. ALPO Time! ALPO Time!

Look at 'em. Every natural instinct tells 'em they should eat meat. And you know something? Their instincts are abosolutely *right*.

Meat is good for dogs. Full of protein, energy, nourishment. I feed my dogs ALPO Beef Chunks Dinner because it's meat by-products,

beef and balanced nutrition.

ALPO's all a dog ever needs to eat.

There's no better dog food in the world.

mer, product, and competition) will aid you in discovering other possible appeals.

Humor—Maybe, Maybe Not

Humor is a very popular device, especially with writers of radio spots. But not all uses of humor are effective. In fact, very few supposedly humorous commercials are genuinely funny. Perhaps humor is a favorite with beginning copywriters because it seems easy to write. But real humor is exceedingly difficult to apply to sales messages. Too many radio writers think of themselves as budding Eddie Murphys or Woody Allens, but unless the funny flair sounds spontaneous and original you run the risk of eliciting groans instead of smiles, and cash registers will ring up "No Sale."

Even spots that titillate on first or second hearing may wear out their welcome quickly. (Who listens to and responds to the same joke after half a dozen hearings?) It is wiser to make your situation or character funny or amusing by writing it in a warm and engaging style and adding just a touch of irony. But make certain that the selling manner doesn't overshadow the selling message.

When producing a humorous spot, cast the voices and direct the tempo with careful regard for timing and inflection. Humor should never sound forced. To succeed, it must be fresh and light.

Imagination—Radio's Big Plus

Imaginations, the writer's and the listener's, work more effectively in radio advertising than in any other medium. The input is all audio: sound effects, voices, and music. As a writer, you are your own art director, and you are not constrained by the space limitations of print or by the linearity of TV. You create mental pictures and activate the imagination of your listeners. With audience attention riveted, interest increases, product points gain emphasis, and your spot is on its way to fulfilling its persuasive function.

In radio, you not only design and set the scene, you also establish time and place—or immediately change them—with your kit of audio tools. In seconds, you can get the listener to picture a caveman in prehistory or a Martian in 2001. In one of Stan Freberg's best radio spots, an "on-the-scene" announcer excitedly described a thousand airplanes flying over Lake Michigan and dropping tons of cherries onto a frothy mountain of whipped cream. The "set" cost nothing. It was simply the product of a rich and bountiful imagination.

Another of radio's most inventive (and award-winning) copywriters, Chuck Blore, claims that there is nothing that cannot be done on radio, at least "visually." According to copywriter Larry Rood: "Radio is the most visual of all media. You can create characters, situations, whole worlds that can't be duplicated on TV or in print. When you create this imaginary situation, the listener can project himself into that world through imagination."

The key words in this passage are "project himself." Your commercial must trigger your listener's imagination, participation, and involvement. Unless your commercial succeeds in this, it won't succeed in meeting its marketing and advertising goals.

TV—Still a New Medium

Commercials on TV have been around for well over three decades, and their creative potential has still not been fully explored. Every day, we see new techniques, such as surrealistic art work and bigger-than-life photography, designed to overwhelm the viewer with a dramatic impression of the product. Technologically, there is little in the way of special effects that you cannot achieve on film or videotape. The exciting fantasies of films like *Star Wars* and *E.T.* are there for use in commercials. Every scene your imagination can envision can be put on film for the world to see. Even scenes your mind can't dream up can be electronically created by computers, which can be programed to generate new forms of graphics and animation. The advent of videotape and "fast film" makes it possible to shoot practically anything, anywhere, at any time, day or night.

The new techniques are exciting, but they are very expensive. Some of them force the cost of commercials into the hundreds of thousands of dollars. The true challenge to the creative person working in TV is to come up with fresh, innovative ideas that do not depend entirely on advanced technology. And the second challenge is to search continually for new film, tape, animation, or stop-motion techniques that are both provocative and relatively inexpensive.

Part of the excitement in television advertising today has been inspired by new commercial forms made possible by the new electronic media. One interesting development in this area is the "infomercial," a commercial intended to provide the kind of in-depth product information that cannot be presented within the time constraints of a 30- or even 60-second commercial. Infomercials (or "advertorials") can run as long as 30 minutes and can therefore accommodate lengthy and detailed explanations and demonstrations of product features, uses, benefits, and advantages. Commercial time of five minutes or more is affordable on cable television because some cable networks direct their programing at small, narrowcast audiences and therefore charge advertisers substantially less for air time. Infomercials can be made for a few thousand dollars, require only the on-camera services of a spokesperson, and can be reused at sales meetings and sent to distributors.

Perhaps more revolutionary is videotex, which basically is a method of running copy (alphanumerics) and graphics on the television screen. With Teletext, a videotex service that is broadcast through the air, consumers can select product information for viewing. Viewdata, another videotex service, but sent over telephone and cable wires, has been used in direct response advertising to elicit orders for products and services by means of an attached control panel and with the assistance of a computer. Both systems can be used to provide advertiser-originated consumer information.

At the present time, these innovations are at a fairly primitive stage of development. However, they already offer new opportunities to advertisers and copywriters. And they will no doubt transform not only the way products are advertised, but the way they are bought and sold.

What Is a "Good" Commercial?

On network TV alone, there were 248,000 commercial units in 1983. And that's just network! And that's before the advent of 15-second unintegrated commercials in 30-second units. Numbers like these mean that one of the principal requirements of a "good" commercial is that it must stand out from the crowd. If it doesn't, obviously the advertiser who's paying the bills is losing his shirt.

Research shows that most people don't mind television or radio advertising in general. What they detest are certain commercial treatments. They don't like to be yelled at or treated rudely. They want to be respected. And that's also what a good commercial should do. It should be a friend rather than an intruder. It should be welcome every time it comes into someone's home.

In addition, a good commercial is honest. It should express the creative strategy in a highly believable manner. If your commercial is insincere or untrue, your customer may spot it in an instant. And even if it takes longer for him to find out that you've been deceptive or misleading or downright dishonest, the result will be the same: declining sales and perhaps irreparable damage to your client's (and your own) reputation.

A good commercial is positive. It should leave your potential customer with a favorable impression of the product. And it should make the viewer or listener feel good about the company that makes the product. Avoid negative implications, and take advantage of every opportunity to show the product and the company in the best possible light.

A good commercial is persuasive. It should get people to buy the product and make them more likely to enjoy it when they use it. Remember, it isn't enough to win prizes. You're not selling yourself, your creative talent, or even your commercial. You're selling your client's product or service. And if you don't persuade the consumer to buy it, you're wasting your time and your client's money.

A good commercial is simple. When audiences hear or see a commercial, they have one question in mind: "What's in it for me?" The less effort they have to expend in getting the answer to this question, the more effort they're likely to use in buying the product. Most commercials are too complicated structurally and too involved verbally. The best advertising craftsmen have one thing in common: a working knowledge of the fine art of omission. They do only what is necessary, and they do that succinctly and competently.

A good commercial is specific. It should make one definite point and support it with concrete evidence. Use numbers if you can. And explain product design or ingredients if they are distinctive or important. Avoid relying on general impressions and vague themes.

A good commercial talks person to person. It should not be addressed to broad demographic groups, such as working women or school children or retirees. It should not even appeal to specific product users, such as car owners or bran cereal buyers. It should talk to *one* man or woman or child who has a problem, and it should show how your product can solve *that* person's problem.

A good commercial makes a promise. Whether it is logical or emotional, however, the promise must be related to the product. It does not have to be in the form of a sentence or a statement. In some cases, a picture will do as well—or better. Or the promise can be suggested or implied by the story you tell or by the tone you convey.

A good commercial builds a personality for the product. Of course, this is a long-term process. But once you have decided on a particular identity or image, stick to it by making sure that every TV or radio spot contributes to it consistently and directly.

A good commercial does the unexpected. If some of the other virtues of good advertising seem obvious to you, remember to combine them with surprise. Too many advertisers cling to outmoded, derivative, or stereotyped forms, as do many timid or unimaginative copywriters and artists. But the goal is not to satisfy the creative person's desire to show his creative prowess.

The commercial should perform the extremely useful task of making certain that the advertiser's product will not be lost in the huge swamp of ho-hum advertising.

A good commercial is something everyone in advertising must constantly work for. However, there is a higher level of advertising, the point at which it stops being a craft and comes as close as it can to being an art. What makes the difference is hard to determine. The operative word, probably, is "vitality." The superior commercial starts out as an inspired idea. Then, almost magically, it takes on a life of its own as it hits the airwaves or the TV screen. And later, long after the commercial has run and the campaign is over, it is still remembered with a certain mixture of awe and appreciation.

Choosing The Format 3

The mind of the television viewer or radio listener is a complex piece of machinery that is capable of being attracted by, paying attention to, and absorbing sales messages. However, there is no reason to assume that at any given time your audience is either ready or willing to watch or hear your commercial.

The mind of your prospective customer may be distracted by worries, needs, or concerns that have nothing to do with your product. He may be so intensely engaged in thinking, planning, day-dreaming, problem-solving, or reminiscing that no selling idea can break through to his consciousness. Or he may be reluctant to accept your request for 30 seconds of his attraction, attention, and absorption because he is hungry or bored or impatiently waiting for his favorite program to resume.

Yet, despite these obstacles, your commercial must somehow do its job. And it must not only capture your prospect's interest, but also fix your selling message in his mind, gain his confidence, and urge him to make a purchase.

Obviously, these objectives can be attained only if your communication is stimulating and relevant and presented in an orderly way. Ideas that are arranged coherently, developed logically, and conveyed clearly are easier to understand, accept, and remember than ideas that are unrelated to each other, randomly ordered, and smothered by an attention-getting style or an obtrusive technique.

The Main Idea

Just as common sense dictates that you should never lift too heavy a weight or carry too many things at the same time, so too must you be careful never to overload a commercial with too many selling facts or too large a variety of styles or techniques. If a commercial tries to use too many ideas, words and pictures will emerge haphazardly and ineffectively. Such a commercial is likely to join the 85 percent of all advertisements that, according to William Bernbach, go completely unnoticed.

The studies of Gallup & Robinson, a prominent research organization, have demonstrated the impor-

tance of presenting simple messages in a clear-cut form. These investigations into commercial effectiveness indicate that viewer and listener recall is lessened when multiple ideas are crammed into a TV or radio message. Keep your commercial singular. And give it a sound structure.

Perhaps it is obvious that a 10-second station-break announcement (or I.D.) should contain only one selling idea. With only eight seconds of audio at your disposal, you have only enough time for a basic claim or selling idea and the product or company name. As you create 20-second, 30-second, minute, and two-minute spots, you will be able to include more entertainment and information. But even in the longer commercials the selling idea is still the prime mover of your prospective customer. A good test of a selling idea, in fact, is to make it work effectively in a short spot. Some ingenious advertisers use the same elements, shortened of course, in their I.D.'s that they use for their longer commercials.

Careful study of the commercial examples in Chapters 6 and 9 will indicate how and where some of today's top creators of commercials implant the main idea, support it, and, in some cases, restate it. From opening fade-in to closing fade-out, the basic selling proposition in the best commercials moves progressively within a carefully chosen format and a tautly conceived structure.

Formats

In this book, the term "format" refers to the major types of commercials. The word "structure" is used to mean temporal sequence or arrangement. Some formats—such as problem-solution, narrative, slice of life, and demonstration—have their own definite structure. You begin with a problem and end with a solution. You tell a story with a beginning, a middle, and an end. You dramatize the discovery of a product feature or consumer benefit. Or you show the step-by-step process of using the product. Other formats can be structured in a variety of ways. And all formats can be done in any style and aided by any technique.

21

Which format should you use? Your decision will depend on a number of considerations: the product or service, the market, the audience, the production budget, the intended number of exposures of the commercial, the competition, and so on. Some structures are better suited to certain kinds of products and are entirely wrong for others. Obviously, a problem-solution structure works best for products that can actually solve problems—laundry detergents, but not designer clothes. A narrative structure, in which a special mood is created, is appropriate for products that appeal to the senses—perfumes, but not hardware. A demonstration can be effective for products whose benefits must be shown rather than described—small kitchen appliances, but usually not such consumer package goods as orange juice, soap, and cat food.

The danger in setting down classifications of commercials by format is that it seems to codify creativity and limit experimentation. So this disclaimer is in order: The formats described on the following pages do not by any means constitute a definitive or exhaustive list.

Furthermore, as you begin to analyze commercials, you will note that some of them use more than one format. (See Exhibits 3-1–3-3.) For example, a basic problem-solution commercial can be set in a fantasy scene and include a brief demonstration of the product. Most of the formats are not mutually exclusive. However, in such cases, one format usually dominates: The other can be treated as an additional—and subordinate—element.

Problem-Solution

The problem-solution format is generally understood to be a story-telling genre. Structurally, the problem must come first, the solution second. And both must be presented dramatically. The problem must seem important and should evoke a negative response from the central actor or actors—worry, fear, discomfort, or dissatisfaction. When the product is introduced, whether it is merely shown or briefly demonstrated, it should solve the problem and result in relief, pleasure, or satisfaction.

The problem-solution format differs from the slice-of-life format in that it focuses on (1) a specific problem—ring around the collar (Wisk), spilled liquids on floors or countertops (Bounty), too much caffeine in regular coffee (Sanka, Brim); (2) a specific product feature that represents the solution—more cleaning power, better absorption, less caffeine; and (3) a specific consumer benefit—no more embarrassment, less work and lower cost, no more caffeine-induced nervousness or edginess.

Appropriate products for the problem-solution format are those that actually *do* something—and presumably do it better: laundry detergents and bleaches, household cleaners, toothpastes, deodorants, and headache remedies. However, products whose primary feature is usually sensorily perceived—that is, products that would otherwise be treated in a slice-of-life format—can be positioned as problem-solvers—bathroom tissue in a longer roll (Scott), soap with high cold cream content (Dove), or low-cholesterol margarine (Fleischmann's). In such cases, the selected feature is usually quantifiable: 50 more sheets, 25% moisturizing cream, made with *pure* vegetable oil.

The problem-solution format differs from the narrative commercial in that the actors might talk directly to the audience, a voice-over announcer might introduce the product, and special-effects devices might be used to enhance the entrance or demonstration of the product. There is little attempt to maintain a particular mood or atmosphere. So, when the point is made—that is, when the problem is either clarified or solved—the problem-solution commercial often breaks from the dramatized situation in order to underscore the selling message. The sell may be "hard," but it can be softened by a humorous treatment. Because the problem-solution structure is so widely used, it must be carefully crafted to avoid the appearance of triteness or sameness.

Slice of Life

The slice-of-life format also lets you develop a "plot" with a beginning, middle, and end. However, the story centers on a discovery about a product or the people who make it, sell it, or service it, not on a problem and its solution.

This format fits products whose product feature is general rather than specific and abstract rather than concrete: reliability (Maytag), good service (Union 76), or high quality (Zenith). In fact, the "problem" in a slice-of-life commercial is often a matter of sense-perception, and the "solution" is often highly subjective. The commercial may begin with a character who expresses a desire for a product that tastes better, feels softer, or looks more attractive. However, this desire need not be articulated. The slice-of-life format requires only that this expressed or unexpressed wish be fulfilled, usually by a discovery either prompted by a friend, a relative, or a neighbor or resulting from accidental trial.

In this kind of commercial, the emphasis is usually on a product feature rather than a consumer benefit. The feature, though shared with other products in the category, may be selected in order to give a parity product—facial tissue, food, soap—a special identity or a special "position" in the marketplace.

Therefore, the commercial may focus on a somewhat indeterminate selling point: "Squeezability" in Charmin bathroom tissues, "mountain-grown" flavor in Folger's coffee, mildness in Palmolive dishwashing liquid, or butter-like taste in Parkay margarine. Furthermore, the product feature may be implied rather than expressed. In a Stroh's beer commercial, for example, the "good-taste" message was dramatized by the sound of an off-stage dog lapping up the contents of a beer bottle that the dog had removed from the refrigerator when asked to do so by its on-stage, card-playing owner. The discovery—that the beer is so good that even dogs can't resist it—had to be inferred by the viewer.

The danger in the slice-of-life format is that the message may be lost because of too much vagueness or indirectness. For this reason, the plot should be simple and clear. Each step in the story should relate to the point that has gone before. Interest should be built gradually, and the outcome should come as a surprise. In addition, if the taste, feel, or look of the product depends on uniqueness of ingredients, structure, or design, this point should be emphasized. If the treatment is humorous, the punch line or visual surprise should relate to the product, its features, or its benefits.

Psychologists recognize that, as a principle of learning, a "rewarded" performance is more likely to be remembered than an unrewarded performance. So make sure that your story relates directly to a consumer interest and that the "discoverer" receives a reward: approval from an employer, gratitude from a spouse, or admiration from a friend.

Narrative

The name of this format is all but self-explanatory. A narrative commercial tells a story. Unlike the slice-of-life commercial, however, it attempts to create a situation that is highly personal, emotionally strong, and deeply involving. In the endeavor to create a mood, the narrative (or story-line) commercial may completely ignore all product features and focus exclusively on a consumer benefit. In fact, even the benefit may be only indirectly related to the product.

The Lowenbrau "Here's to Good Friends" and "Miller Time" beer commercials identify their products with leisure, relaxation, and good fellowship. AT&T's "Reach Out and Touch Someone" campaign associated long-distance phone calling with the intimacies of close friendship and strong family ties. Campbell's "Soup for Lunch" spots said nothing about the taste, price, nutritional value, or even quality of the product. They stressed the special warmth of mother-son relationships aided by a midday serving of hot soup.

The narrative commercial may deal with a problem, as in the Hallmark card spots in which a dreary day was made brighter by the receipt of a greeting card from a friend or relative. However, the problem is often emotional—frustration, loneliness, disappointment—and the soft-sell solution may be communicated in a smile, a handshake, or a pat on the back, rather than a summary of product features or consumer benefits, which usually comes at the end of a problem-solution commercial. In an award-winning spot for Coca-Cola, for example, a young fan asked football star "Mean Joe"

Green for his autograph, got turned down, offered Joe a Coke, and got a smile and a T-shirt in return. The features (tasty and thirst-quenching), as well as the benefits (satisfaction and refreshment), were submerged under the less tangible but more touching aura of gratitude and human decency.

Because the narrative format rests so heavily on atmosphere, every attempt must be made to sustain the emotion-generating "feel" of the commercial. The spot should begin and end with the story intact. And the concluding product-identifying voice-over or jingle must not break the spell. Unlike the slice-of-life commercial, this type calls for little or no dialogue, understated acting, and characters who not only induce audience identification, but also create sympathy and elicit involvement.

Demonstration

Television provides the unique opportunity to do what no other mass communication medium can do: show actual proof of a product performance claim. From the very beginning, TV advertising has taken advantage of this opportunity. In the 1950s, a device for slicing and dicing and otherwise preparing vegetables for cooking was frequently demonstrated on late-night television. More recently, similar products—such as the Cuisinart, as well as personal computers and office copiers—have been demonstrated in primetime.

Effective demonstrations hold attention, prove a product's workability or superiority, and convince the viewer to buy. And, of course, they score extremely well in terms of audience involvement. In fact, there's no better way to overcome sales resistance. All research shows this. Nothing sells a prospective customer faster and more compellingly than actually showing him that a product does what it is supposed to do.

Demonstrations are particularly appropriate for products that are genuinely different from others and whose difference is in *how they work,* rather than in how they look, taste, or feel. The commercial can show the product in action, if this is the product's strongest selling point. Or it can focus on a variety of applications, if this is the thrust of the sales message.

However, the demonstration is not limited to technological wonders that perform extraordinary feats, such as hand-held vacuum cleaners, torture-tested wristwatches, and high-speed office copiers. This format can also be used to demonstrate special features of ordinary products, such as thickness in catsup, lack of greasiness in potato chips, and durability in kitchen utensils.

The only requirement is that the feature or benefit be *demonstrated* rather than explained, either by straightforward filming or taping or by time-lapse or before/after photography for slow-working products, such as house paints, grass seed, microwave ovens, and cake mixes. A *discussion* of how something works—because of its ingredients, structure, or design—is not a demonstration.

One cautionary word. If you use a demonstration, you must be absolutely certain that your performance claim is true and that the demonstration itself is authentic.

Product Alone

Showing the product by itself can mean an easy-to-produce and therefore relatively low-cost commercial. You let the viewer look at the product—presumably because it is beautiful, new, or different—while the voice-over announcer tells what it is, what it has (or doesn't have), and what it does.

However, because few products can sustain 30 or 60 seconds of visual attention, advertisers often turn to camera or computer tricks to hold interest. In the early days of television, before time-lapse photography and computer-generated visuals, a woman attired in an oversized pack of Old Gold cigarettes (only her legs showed) tap-danced her way into the hearts and lungs of America. The connection between product and commercial content was tenuous, but the spot had considerable staying power because it offered an unusual variation on the product-alone format.

This format can be used for products that have some "inherent drama," such as new products, old products in a new form or package, or products that are pleasing to the eye. When Contac cold-remedy capsules were introduced, the TV commercials showed, in slow motion and close-up, "tiny time pills" spilling out of a capsule. Burger King filled the TV screen with a shot of the Whopper, followed by a series of vignettes showing each ingredient of the sandwich.

Perfumes have flowed gently out of their artfully designed bottles; models have gracefully descended spiral staircases in mink coats; and Michelob beer, accompanied by minimal voice-over copy, has been dramatically poured into a pilsner glass to the strains of a triumphant melody, for which the only lyric was the repeated word "Michelob."

When the product or package innovation requires explanation, the voice-over announcer can describe the product in detail. Alternatively, when visual appeal is emphasized, the commercial may begin or end with a theme-statement and allow the strong video to do the talking. Burger King, for example, began with the statement that the following presentation of the Whopper was intended to test the power of hungry viewers to resist the appetizing allure of the hamburger. The close: "We hope we won't have to do this again." Michelob beer concluded its slow-motion video with the tag "Some things speak for themselves."

Table-top spots (in which the product is shown on top of a kitchen table) can go with minimal copy, as in some cereal commercials, or with extensive description, as in food commercials offering free recipes.

Although radio may seem to be an unlikely medium for "showing" the product alone, it *can* work for products whose primary use is auditory: recording equipment, records and tapes, concerts, and stereo components. However, radio has also been used to transmit the sound of beer pouring, car engines humming, and soft drinks fizzing. Whenever the sound of a product is easily recognizable, it can be transmitted on radio. In fact, some products that have become identified with a unique sound—Alka-Seltzer (plop, plop, fizz, fizz) and Kellogg's Rice Krispies (snap, crackle, and pop)—are particularly good candidates for product-alone radio treatment.

A subcategory of the product-alone format is the analogy, in which either the product or the use of the product is presented analogically or symbolically. An analogy is defined as "a relation of likeness between two things." The likeness is not between the things themselves, however, but between "two or more attributes, circumstances, or effects." In an analogical commercial, you would use something with a quality or attribute that relates to your product. Bulls have been used to symbolize the "power" of malt liquor and the upswinging stock market for an investment firm. Drinking a rosé wine has been compared to "taking a trip to Portugal." The speed and sleekness of a car have been compared to those qualities in a race horse. For the viewer to make the (sometimes implicit) connection, the analogy must be clear and relevant. Audiences are often unwilling to exert the effort that is necessary to follow a complicated comparison, so the analogy should be relatively simple and logically, as well as emotionally, acceptable.

Spokesman

The use of an on-camera announcer to speak directly to television viewers about a sponsor's product dates from the first days of television. In its simplest form, it is a straight radio announcement illustrated by a moving picture of an announcer and the product. Although it is sometimes enlivened by a demonstration, it is basically "talk," which may be fast and hard sell or personal and intimate.

Direct communication between a spokesperson and the audience is a valuable and generally economical device. The message is straightforward and simple; there is little to distract the viewer or listener from learning about the product and finding out why he or she should buy it. The spokesperson may discuss product features or consumer benefits. Or he may present the product in a problem-solution structure.

Whatever the formal structure may be, this type of commercial has the force of the spokesperson's personality behind it. Many effective network commercials use a "name" announcer. Ed McMahon built a career out of his ability to project sincerity and personal conviction about products. These are the qualities that give this format its selling strength.

The spokesperson can be a salesperson representing the sponsor, the president of the company, or an actor or actress playing either. Lee Iacocca, head of Chrysler Corp., has been an effective spokesman for his company. Airlines and automakers have used a variety of actual employees to discuss the virtues of their products or services.

The spokesperson can also be an expert—say, a nutritionist, a car mechanic, a dishwasher—or, again, an actor or actress playing these roles. He or she can be a well-known movie star, astronaut, or professional athlete. Here, however, product and spokesperson must be carefully matched. Sexy film stars touting auto transmissions or hardware products may not be as effective as celebrities who can be identified with the product (British actor Robert Morley for British Airways), seem to be likely users (Olympic gymnast Cathy Rigby for Tampons), or come across as authority figures (Lauren Bacall and John Houseman).

The personality-spokesperson is an actor or actress who plays a role written especially for the product. This variant relies on a performer (often a comedian or comic actor) who can command attention and interest with a distinctive characterization—a unique voice, delivery, or appearance.

Testimonial

Word-of-mouth advertising is one of the most effective ways of calling attention to a product. It comes from people who have used a product and liked it. The testimonial is an attempt to capture the persuasiveness of this kind of advertising. Like the spokesperson, the testifier speaks directly to the audience. However, instead of talking about the product, he discusses his experience with it.

Testimonials can be delivered by either celebrities or ''unknowns.'' Famous people can give your commercial special appeal. And if the spot as a whole is informative, entertaining, and promising, the extra cost can be worth it. Again, however, product and testifier must ''go together.'' The viewer or listener must believe that the celebrity has actually used the product and is really expressing his or her own feelings about it. In a testimonial/demonstration, basketball star Wilt Chamberlain showed that he was a Volkswagen user by getting into a VW ''Bug,'' driving it without bumping his head against the roof or his knees against the steering wheel, and thus demonstrating that at least one small car was roomy enough for even seven-footers.

On the other hand, an unknown person who recommends a product is probably less subject to the suspicion that he or she is merely endorsing the product for a fee. Furthermore, audiences often respond favorably to peer recommendations. An ''average'' consumer in a store, a home, or a garage can recommend a detergent, a rug cleaner, or an oil filter and create credibility.

In 1982, after several bottles of Tylenol pain-reliever capsules were found to be laced with strychnine and the product was pulled from drug store and supermarket shelves nationwide, the company presented a series of testimonials featuring responsible-looking wives and mothers who convincingly underlined the PR-motivated campaign theme: trust. As far as the audience could tell, these women were long-time users of the product. And their naturalness and sincerity helped restore Tylenol to its position as category leader.

A testimonial can be structured in narrative, slice-of-life, or problem-solution form. The camera can be hidden to catch spontaneity and convey authenticity. The commercial can also be presented as an interview. When the testifier uses his own words, the testimony is more plausible and persuasive.

Musical

In television, the musical consists of a vocal or instrumental sound track accompanied by a performance of the music, either just singing or both singing and dancing. In radio, it is only a song. In both media, the music should be catchy and upbeat—attention-getting and entertaining. The lyrics can describe a product feature, as in a TWA fare-reduction campaign called ''Come Fly with Me,'' or tout a consumer benefit, as in New York City's ''I Love New York'' spots.

No product is especially well suited to musical treatment, except perhaps musical products, such as records, music videos, stage shows, rock concerts, and symphonic or operatic productions. The format best fits any product that at a particular time seems to need a splashy, spectacular presentation. Thus, many product introductions, revivals, and repositionings have been set to elaborate song-and-dance numbers. And the same is true of products undergoing a special promotion—sweepstakes, price cuts, and special events (especially holiday celebrations).

Nevertheless, certain mass-appeal, quasi-parity products, such as soft drinks and fast food, have turned to the musical format again and again. RC Cola ran a series of narrative-video/musical-audio spots under the theme ''Me and My RC.'' Coca-Cola had a large, international-looking group of children line up along a horizon and sing, ''I'd like to buy the world a Coke.'' Dr Pepper used a lead singer/dancer and a group of spectators (who finally got into the act) to urge its youthful target market to ''Be a Pepper.''

The jingle is a miniature version of the musical, and its brevity requires that it be used as a framing device or as a closing signature. However, music can also be used to enhance a dramatic moment in an emotionally engaging narrative or to create atmosphere for any kind of dramatization. When the characters in a narrative actually act out the lyrics of a song and the song runs the entire length of the spot, the commercial is a musical because the audio determines the content of the video. When the music, whether vocal or instrumental, supports the story, the commercial is what it is by virtue of its video content.

To Sum Up

One final warning about formats: The aforementioned types cover the territory fairly well. However, the most common commercial on television is not adequately described by any of them. It is a combination of continuous music, voice-over narration, and storytelling video. The latter is usually a series of vignettes that fall into the slice-of-life or problem-solution category. The difficulty with such commercials is not that they are unclassifiable. It is that they are too cluttered, burdened as they are with too many elements, each of which fights for attention and none of which dominates.

Too often, the result is a commercial that is unclear and ineffective.

Make it easy for your prospective viewer or listener. Choose a format or a combination of formats. But develop the ad clearly and logically. Don't weigh it down with too many ideas or elements. Remember that the format itself will neither compel nor sell. But as you develop your selling idea within the framework of a format, don't add too much. Keep the sales message in the forefront of your mind and in the foreground of your commercial.

When you have the opportunity to spend a few hours watching TV or listening to the radio, notice and evaluate each commercial's format. Note which ones have well-defined formats and which ones do not. The best-remembered and most effective spots will usually be those with strong selling ideas and well-chosen formats.

Exhibit 3-1. Mixed Formats: S.O.S

Advertiser: Miles Laboratories, Inc.

Agency: Doyle Dane Bernbach, Inc.

Product: S.O.S scouring pads

Title: "New York Ladies"

Formats: Slice of life/Demonstration/Comparison

Length: 30 seconds

(SFX: CLANG OF POT)
S.O.S LADY: (OFF CAMERA) Grace is that you?

BRILLO LADY: No, it's Miss America. I'm here doing dishes between appearances.

S.O.S LADY: (LAUGHS) Still with the jokes. Listen, did you get S.O.S?
BRILLO LADY: No.

S.O.S LADY: No!? But I told you it's better than Brillo.
BRILLO LADY: I know.

S.O.S LADY: The soap lasts longer.
BRILLO LADY: I know.

S.O.S LADY: And it cuts grease quicker than Brillo.
BRILLO LADY: I know.

S.O.S LADY: So, Grace, S.O.S could get you out of the kitchen faster.

(SFX: CRUNCH!!!)

BRILLO LADY: Who wants to get out of the kitchen faster?

Exhibit 3-2. Mixed Formats: WICO

Advertiser: WICO Corp.

Agency: Bentley, Barnes & Lynn, Inc.

Product: WICO joysticks

Title: "Whacko over WICO"

Formats: Slice of life/Musical/Demonstration

Length: 30 seconds

1. SONG: YOUR STICKO WON'T GO WHACKO WHEN IT'S A WICO.

2. BOY: Wow! I'm scoring at home like I've never scored. I'm whacko over Wico.

3. SONG: YOUR STICKO WON'T GO WHACKO WHEN IT'S A WICO.

4. TEEN BOY: They're as tough as the joy sticks at the arcade.

5. TEEN GIRL: He's whacko over Wico.

6. ANNCR VO: Wico...the only authentic arcade joy sticks.

7. The most durable...most accurate...the fastest controls money can buy.

8. MOM: I've been practicing.

9. DAD: She's whacko over Wico.

10. SONG: YOUR STICKO WON'T GO WHACKO WHEN IT'S A WICO.

Exhibit 3-3. Mixed Formats: Union 76

Advertiser: Union Oil Co. of California　　Title: "Thanks, Nick"

Agency: Leo Burnett U.S.A.　　Formats: Spokesman/Slice of Life/Musical

Product: Union 76 Unleaded Regular gasoline　　Length: 60 seconds

---

SING: YOU'RE ROLLIN' DOWN THE HIGHWAY

THERE'S SO MUCH OUT THERE TO SEE

NICK: Hi, I'm Nick, from Murph's Seventy-Six. And I'm hearing a lot of "Thank-You's" lately.

VOICE 1: Hey, Nick, thanks! You saved me money!

NICK: See?

VOICE 2: Yeah, Nick--I really didn't need premium unleaded to quiet those knocks and pings! Thanks, buddy.

NICK: Noo problem. Oh, the reason for the "Thank-You's" is Union Seventy-Six Unleaded Regular. It's the unleaded with the big plus...more spirit. Seventy-Six Unleaded has more spirit than other unleaded regulars.

VOICE 3: Thanks, Nick!

NICK: Anytime! Listen, if your car's knocking and pinging and you're thinkin' you might have to pay for premium unleaded...try Union Seventy-Six Unleaded Regular instead. You'll recognize it by the big plus on the pump. It tells you about the big plus that's been inside our gasoline for a long time...more spirit. Try it...you might thank me, too.

SEXY FEMALE: Thanks, Nick...

NICK: Sure...gulp...You're welcome...

SING: COME IN AND GO WITH THE SPIRIT

THE SPIRIT OF SEVENTY-SIX

Structure, Style & Technique 4

After you have decided to use one format or a combination of formats, you must make a number of other decisions about your radio or television commercial. The format is only the large framework within which you will work. Still to be chosen are the structure (which may be determined by the format), the style, and the techniques you will use to enhance your selling message.

Of course, just to make the decision-making process a little more complicated, you need not begin by choosing a format. Your commercial idea may well have been inspired by the punch line of a joke, an intriguing print ad, or the refrain from a popular song—in which case you could well begin with a style (humor), a technique (computer graphics), or a musical idea. The important goal is not to start at a particular stage in the creative process, but to start *somewhere* and then to consider all the formal, structural, stylistic, and technical options in a relatively systematic or orderly way.

Structure

A commercial that presents its message within a particular structure—a logical sequence of related facts, impressions, and scenes—has a better chance of making its audience react favorably and profitably. Structure is the backbone of your sales message. It establishes continuity in the action and coherence among the parts. Rather than restricting a viewer's or listener's understanding and interest, a unified structure, imaginatively conceived, actually helps him follow your logic or get involved in your story and remember your message.

In a continuing research study for an important TV advertiser, this fact stood out: Commercials with strong, well-defined structures registered much more powerfully than those in which there was little or no design. The better-structured commercials were not only better remembered; they were also superior in influencing the decision to buy.

As we stated in Chapter 3, some formats have their own unique structure, their own special way of arranging scenes or events. The problem-solution format requires a presentation of the problem followed by a presentation of the solution. In the slice-of-life commercial, the main character or characters move from a state of ignorance about the product, through a product test or trial, to a state of awareness of and satisfaction with the product. The narrative format follows a strict story-telling scheme. And the demonstration necessarily presents the product as it actually works in a step-by-step process.

The other formats—product alone, spokesperson, testimonial, and musical—usually focus on a single product feature or consumer benefit. When several features or benefits are treated, it is sometimes useful to proceed from least to most important, or vice versa.

In addition, any of these formats can use a structure ordinarily identified with a different format: problem-solution, ignorance-trial-awareness, story, or demonstration. However, the presenter-spokesperson-testifier *discusses* the problem and its solution, takes the *audience* through the discovery process, or *tells* a story of product use. The musical—uniquely—is adaptable to any structure, including demonstration, which can be performed by singers and dancers or animated figures.

Vignettes

Besides these standard structures, there are many other methods of arranging material in a radio or television commercial. The form called "vignettes" is a series of brief scenes in which the same action is performed or the same characters perform different actions. Diet Pepsi used a number of short glimpses of slim and attractive people, with musical accompaniment, to show the visible benefits offered by a low-calorie soft drink. Alka-Seltzer presented a series of close-up shots focusing on a variety of stomachs adversely affected by overeating and overdrinking. Benson & Hedges humorously acknowledged the difficulties of adjusting to a 100mm cigarette by showing product users accidentally breaking their cigarettes against windows, mirrors, and walls. And True Value demonstrated the various ways in which its worktable could be used by do-it-yourself homeowners.

In these cases, the commercials consisted almost entirely of vignettes, with the product making an appearance either intermittently or at the end. However, the vignettes were—as they almost always are—used *within* a problem-solution, slice-of-life, or demonstration format.

This structure fits products that can be used in different ways, appeal to a variety of people, or rest on one very specific selling point that bears repeating. It seems to be most effective with a self-explanatory video, minimal voice-over, and a strong music track.

Comparison

When the product or service is demonstrably superior to, or at least different from, its competitors, a "comparison" might be in order. This structure can work three ways. First, you can show the "other" product or products and then show your own. Second, you can show the products performing side by side. Third, you can show the products in a series of alternating scenes.

In a Hefty bag spot, Jonathan Winters played a garbage collector who first suffered the inconvenience of having the competitor's bag burst and then demonstrated the "extra" strength of Hefty's product. Both Heinz and Scott have subjected their catsup and toilet tissue, respectively, to side-by-side comparisons. And in alternating shots of McDonald's, Wendy's, and its own methods, Burger King revealed how different fast-food hamburgers are prepared for consumption.

A variation of the side-by-side comparison is the head-to-head test, in which two competing products are tried by actors or actual consumers. Pepsi-Cola aired a series of commercials representing the results of a nationwide competition with Coca-Cola. Similarly, margarine has been tested against butter, and cars have been tested against each other for gas mileage and other features.

Continuing Series

The "continuing series" is a larger structural form in which the same characters or the same situation appears in one commercial after another. Like vignettes, the series usually focuses on one or, at most, two product attributes. It is particularly effective for "reminder" advertising—that is, when the product is well established and requires only the restatement of a simple campaign theme to sell the product. Probably, many continuing series are not planned for in advance but are developed as a result of one commercial's unusual success or because of the popularity of one or more of its characters.

The most elaborate example of this type of commercial is the durable Miller Lite beer series featuring Rodney Dangerfield and a host of sports celebrities. The campaign actually began with single spokespersons, such as football star Bubba Smith, touting two consumer benefits: "less filling" and "tastes great."

This format evolved into a slice-of-life dialogue between two sports figures, each defending a different benefit. Eventually, the two-person argument moved out of the tavern and turned into a sometimes more than verbal battle between two groups made up of participants in earlier spots. By 1984, the Miller Brewing Co. had fielded two baseball teams, hosted a celebrity "roast," and sponsored a cookout—all with the same large cast of Lite veterans and the same "less filling/ tastes great" exchange.

Style

As the dictionary indicates, the word "style" derives from the Latin *stilus,* originally a writing instrument. Handwriting style is affected by the instrument you use and the way you use it. Commercial style is similarly expressed by the *manner* in which you present your material—how you hear it or see it and how you want it to be heard or seen. Style is a reflection of a perspective or a point of view. Every commercial has one. The goal is to make a choice from among the varieties of style and then to stick to it. Consistent style is as important as clear message and logical structure.

Comedy & Tragedy

The most obvious categories of style are the comic and the tragic. The latter is seldom used in radio and TV commercials because audiences tend to ignore or forget products or services that are associated with disturbing or depressing themes. They would rather be lifted up than let down. Of course, the difficulty is often unavoidable if the product or service deals with personal tragedy—death, fire, burglary, or disease. Thus, insurance companies, fire-alarm manufacturers, security-system makers, and healthcare facilities must almost always take the risk. However, the tragic events inevitably portrayed, discussed, or at least mentioned are usually subsumed under the problem-solution format, and the final emphasis is on the solution that is available through purchase of the product or service.

Far more numerous are the radio and television spots that use humor in one way or another. In fact, many commercials are actually adaptations of standard stage, film, and TV comedy forms, such as comic sketches, situation comedies, standup monologues, and comic/straight-man routines. And many of the spots that are not full-blown adaptations of established comedic forms use some kind of humor, including slapstick, puns, jokes, and comic characters.

Comic sketches are problem-solution or slice-of-life commercials in which one or more characters act out a more or less real-life situation that ends in a joke— often at the expense of the main character. In a Wendy's commercial, one of the most successful comic sketches ever written, former manicurist Clara Peller stood at a competitor's fast-food counter, examined the huge hamburger bun and the tiny hamburger in it, and asked repeatedly, "Where's the beef?" Because of her unique delivery and distinctive voice, Peller gained national attention. And "Where's the beef?" became a household phrase, as well as a customer password at Wendy's restaurants.

Situation comedies are commercials (usually slice of life) in which the same characters in the same comic situation appear again and again. The principal characters—Bill Cosby (Jell-O), Murph (Union 76), and the Maytag repairman—ordinarily participate in slight variations of the same joke.

Standup monologues are often delivered by well-known comedians, such as George Burns, Rodney Dangerfield, and Jonathan Winters. The performer is often a spokesperson. But whether he speaks for the product directly or promotes it indirectly by falling victim to the competitor's "shoddy" product, he must bring distinctiveness to the role, which he does, ordinarily, by caricaturing a particular personality type. Straight-man/comic routines have been performed by James Garner and Mariette Hartley for Polaroid, Ray Goulding and Bob Elliot for a variety of products, and such well-known comedy teams as Stiller and Meara, the Smothers Brothers, and Rowan and Martin. Typically, one actor plays Don Quixote (idealistic, naive, or gullible), and the other plays Sancho Panza (realistic, sophisticated, or wary).

Humor can be crossed with fantasy, as in the animated Star-Kist spots with Charlie the Tuna and in a Fruit of the Loom men's underwear commercial that showed a group of men dressed up as different kinds of fruit. Humor can also be used with special effects. In an IBM spot starring a Charlie Chaplin look-alike, the film was run in fast motion to create the effect of a silent film and to suggest the frenetic activity required by running a business without the help of a computer. Federal Express showed a series of fast-talking package senders who had used the "wrong" air-courier service and were trying to explain why their packages were late. The audio was speeded up so as to be almost unintelligible.

Satire is a special form of humor in which a play (*Romeo and Juliet, A Streetcar Named Desire*), a movie (*Gone with the Wind, Casablanca*), a personality (Humphrey Bogart, Fidel Castro), or an event (the first moon landing, Columbus's discovery of America) is mocked or parodied. Naturally, the object of the satire must be widely known, and the treatment must unequivocally relate the commercial to its source.

The problem is that besides a small number of Old Testament stories (Adam and Eve, Samson and Delilah, Jonah and the whale), four or five Shakespeare plays, and such familiar works of art as the Venus de Milo, the Mona Lisa, and Grant Wood's *American Gothic,* few literary or artistic creations will do. However, subliterary works—comic books (*Superman, Batman, Wonder Woman*), fairy tales, popular songs, block-buster films *(Star Wars, Rocky),* comic strips ("Little Orphan Annie," "Peanuts"), and TV programs with exceptionally high ratings—are frequently used for satirical purposes.

Experience shows that a well-crafted comedy-commercial can be a powerful selling medium. However, humor is not a universal panacea. First, it is too often used as an easy way out of an advertising dilemma that could have been better solved by the use of a different kind of treatment. The fact is, as we suggested earlier, some products are ill-suited to comedy. Second, even if the product or service is appropriate for this style, the selling idea must be well integrated into the commercial. Otherwise, the spot may be very entertaining, but not very successful. Third, the humor must be readily understandable. It cannot be based on a highbrow novel, a seldom-seen foreign film, or a local or regional personality or event. Fourth, the humor must be inoffensive. It cannot insult *any* member of the audience, particularly minority groups. And most advertisers avoid using persons, places, things, or even words that are regarded as sacred by a religious group (e.g., a rabbi, the Vatican, prayer, the Koran, communion, "miracle"). And fifth, the humor must "wear" under constant repetition. There's nothing more boring than a joke you've heard before.

Fantasy & Documentary

Two other contrasting categories of style are fantasy and documentary. The latter, less often used, tries to create a slice-of-life atmosphere that suggests spontaneous, unrehearsed, and therefore "realistic" dialogue and/or action. Usually, a voice-over announcer describes the scene, which may be a demonstration of the product, a trial use, or a dramatization of a problem. This style can also be used for supermarket, on-the-street, or shopping mall interviews. When the product speaks for itself—when it is genuinely new or different, solves a serious problem, or performs an important task or function—the no-nonsense approach, without frills or fanfare, can be very effective. In other words, if the goal of the commercial is solely to *inform,* the documentary may be the best style in which to present it.

When your message is less definite or less earth-shaking—that is, when you are dealing with a parity product that appeals to the senses—you might want to go to the other extreme: fantasy. Successful fantasy campaigns have used animated green giants, "real" white knights, and other characters and special effects to create a make-believe world. In such a world, the product can be made, grown, used, or consumed—happily and contentedly.

Fantasy works because audiences have been conditioned to accept it since early childhood, a fact well noted by advertisers of children's products, such as pre-sweetened cereal, toys, fast food, and computer games. A fantasy ad can appeal to almost anyone because of its charm or warmth or humor. However, you must never lose sight of the selling proposition or the product. Even though you suspend a viewer's or listener's disbelief, your purpose is to idealize the product—not provide a temporary diversion.

Fantasy can be divided into four types: the imaginary, the far away, the futuristic, and the nostalgic. The "imaginary" includes almost all animated commercials (Green Giant vegetables, Keebler cookies, Star-Kist tuna) and spots in which animals talk or fantasy figures (leprechauns, witches, unicorns) appear.

The "far away" fantasy uses such settings as rural scenes, mountains, European cities, jungles, deserts, the Arctic, and any unfamiliar terrain or locale—especially when it is idealized or romanticized. In the "futuristic" style, the commercial may simply use a setting drawn from an imaginary future—inside an intergalactic space bus or in a 21st-century city. Apple Computer introduced its Macintosh model in a spot based on George Orwell's futuristic novel, *1984*. In this controversial commercial (Did it "sell" or merely entertain?), a woman athlete ran through a seated throng of uniformed figures hypnotically gazing at "Big Brother" on a television screen. After the woman smashed the tube with a sledgehammer, the voice-over underscored the conventional-versus-revolutionary theme of the spot.

"Nostalgic" commercials use the past rather than the future. Marlboro retargeted its cigarettes from women to men by using the American West as a context for its enduring campaign. Pepperidge Farm used a horse-drawn delivery wagon and a grandfatherly delivery man, all in a turn-of-the-century setting, to sell its bakery products.

In addition, regardless of how it departs from the here and now, any fantasy commercial can be given a surrealistic treatment. In this style, images are distorted, idealized, or exaggerated—usually by camera tricks or with computer-generated graphics. Chanel advertised its No. 5 perfume in a campaign that featured thematically unrelated images. The stark but romantic scene was underscored by the line "Share the fantasy." Levi Strauss created a series of spots made up of computerized visuals that presented a gravity-defying landscape populated by levitating figures and objects. Both of these dreamy, highly evocative campaigns created alluring fantasy worlds to which sweet scents and prewashed jeans, respectively, promised to provide easy entry.

Technique

By "technique," we mean not just "a method for accomplishing a desired aim," but a *technical* method that depends on the use of mechanical equipment. Techniques are necessary whenever you must simulate either the video or audio portion of a commercial. You may need special sound effects—cars crashing, waves roaring, or assembly lines humming—that require either on-location recording, which may be too costly, or a reasonable facsimile. Or you may want to show a process—food digesting, a headache disappearing, or grass growing—that cannot be filmed because it is either internal or invisible or cannot be shown in 30 seconds because it stretches out over a much longer period of time. In such cases, animation, special recording equipment, unusual camera angles or lenses, or computer-controlled cameras may be useful.

Animation

Until very recently, the production technique that most completely liberated the imaginations of copywriters and art directors was animation. This is so because virtually *anything* can be made to happen in animated commercials. Ordinary-looking people can perform superhuman feats. Animals can sing and dance. And even inanimate objects can be given human attributes and abilities. As a result, many products have acquired animal spokespersons. Solutions to such problems as stained teeth, tired feet, and stuffy noses can be dramatized vividly and graphically. And characters (as well as objects) can be made to "perform" exactly to the specifications of writers, artists, and directors.

Animation in commercials has been influenced by every animated-filmmaker from Walt Disney to Ralph Bakshi and by cartoonists from Charles Gould to Gary Trudeau. The technique can be used to create a cartoon story in the slice-of-life format, a package logo brought to life with highly stylized drawings, or an abstract design that underscores a selling theme or enhances the visual appeal of a product. Animation can be achieved by moving stills, in which still photographs are shot in different ways to achieve the effect of movement, or by stop motion, in which three-dimensional figures (Speedy Alka-Seltzer and the Pillsbury doughboy) are photographed one frame at a time to simulate movement. Otherwise, animation requires that each of the 24 frames per second be drawn individually.

Animated commercials are popular because they are entertaining. And that is simultaneously their strength and weakness. If you have real "news" to communicate—about price, quality, or availability—it is often best just to say so. Entertainment may be a distraction. Also, if your message is very personal, you may want to avoid this potentially charming but somewhat impersonalizing technique. It is difficult for viewers to identify with cartoon characters. If you need to attract attention, however, if your sales idea would be enhanced by an entertaining presentation, or if your target audience is very young, you might want to consider using animation.

Keep in mind, too, that animation embraces more than cartoons. It can be used to show a complicated process simply and clearly. It also allows you to reveal how products work in ways or places that are unfilmable or unphotographable—that is, when their operation is microscopic, when they work inside the body, or when the problem they solve might be more tastefully presented symbolically rather than actually (e.g., toilet bowl stains, body odor).

Yet again, because animation is expensive, it should be used carefully and selectively. If you need to demonstrate something that can't be demonstrated in any other way, use animation. Or if you think the fantasy achievable through animation fits your product and message, use it. However, if you can do nearly as good a job without investing the extra time and money required by this technique, try something else.

Computer Graphics

Since the early 1970s, a new form of animation has broadened the horizons of advertising people far beyond the seemingly infinite possibilities offered by the original form. Unlike the hand-drawn variety, this type of animation is mechanically generated by the use of computer-controlled cameras. In this technique, the color and movement that otherwise require the drawing of every frame can be generated from one piece of black-and-white art. Each frame of film can be layered with any number of superimposed images. And three-dimensional objects can be moved, rotated, and distorted in any conceivable way. The result of all this is a visually spectacular end-product in which images contract, expand, explode, implode, and undergo dazzling transformations that are impossible to achieve by other means.

Among the first successful computer commercials was a fantasy spot for 7UP that focused exclusively on a winged woman who floated above multicolored bubbles and amidst fountains of bright lights and other pyrotechniques. The visual drama created by this eye-catching and eye-holding scene was entirely sufficient to maintain viewer interest and involvement. Additional action or explanatory voice-over were completely unnecessary.

Another outstanding example of computer-generated effects is a TRW spot based on Martin Escher's optical-illusion paintings in which objects are transformed into other objects through subtle gradations of form and color. In this commercial, a bird was shown to be part of an interlocking pattern of birds. In turn, the spaces between the birds became fish. And, from a more distant perspective, birds and fish were seen to be dots in a photograph of a man's face.

The same advantages and disadvantages apply to computer as to hand-drawn animation. On the one hand, it is an entertaining technique that can attract and hold interest. On the other hand, although it creates a more or less abstract or symbolic or "unreal" universe in which incredible things happen, it is also quite impersonal. And the temptation to achieve artistic perfection or show off technical virtuosity is almost as strong

for advertisers as it is for writers, artists, and technicians. One way to solve the problem of impersonality is to combine computer graphics with live footage of real things and people, as NCR did in a spot featuring both a revolving polyhedron and vignettes of company workers and products displayed on each geometrical facet of the turning globe. Used in the station-break logos of all the major networks, computer graphics seem to be especially good for corporate advertising in which an image of technological sophistication is the campaign theme.

Special Effects

In radio, special effects include all the simulated sounds that can be reproduced with real objects (e.g., doors closing, shoes walking) and special recording equipment. In TV, special effects include all these, as well as simulated visual effects achieved by special cameras, unusual camera techniques, special processing equipment, and editing.

Basically, the purpose of special effects is to create an illusion. Backgrounds can be created by "back projection," or projecting a moving or still picture on a translucent screen that gives the effect of a "real" set behind the actors and props. The illusion of a wild animal crashing through a wall (Schlitz), a businessman flying through an airport (Hertz), or an animated character sitting on top of a real car (Rusty Jones) can be achieved by "matting," in which two different scenes are shot separately and later combined into one. Shots can be taken from different perspectives and combined. Objects can be miniaturized as models to create the effect of a shipwreck, a flood, or a fire. Various lenses can be used to soften the focus, stretch the visual image, or otherwise distort the picture. Two or more different scenes can be shown on the screen at the same time ("split screen"). Product entrances and exits can be enhanced by fades (both in and out). Film can be speeded up ("fast motion"), slowed down ("slow motion"), reversed, or frozen. The possibilities are almost limitless.

While special effects are sometimes necessary and often useful, they can, like other commercial enhancements—including style—clutter up the listening or viewing experience or provide an easy, but unsatisfactory, way out of a tough communication problem. It cannot be said often enough that no technique should be used unless it dramatizes, clarifies, underscores, or in some way enhances the selling idea. After all, special effects are, as the name implies, *special*. And they are not to be employed unless they fulfill a special need or solve a special problem. To be used effectively, they must be chosen carefully and integrated smoothly into the commercial. (For good examples of the successful integration of special effects and other commercial elements, see Exhibits 4-1—4-3).

Exhibit 4-1. Integrating Elements: Green Giant

Advertiser: Green Giant Co.

Agency: Leo Burnett Co.

Product: Green Giant beans and corn

Title: "Bean/Nib"

Format: Slice of life/Animation/Music

Length: 60 seconds

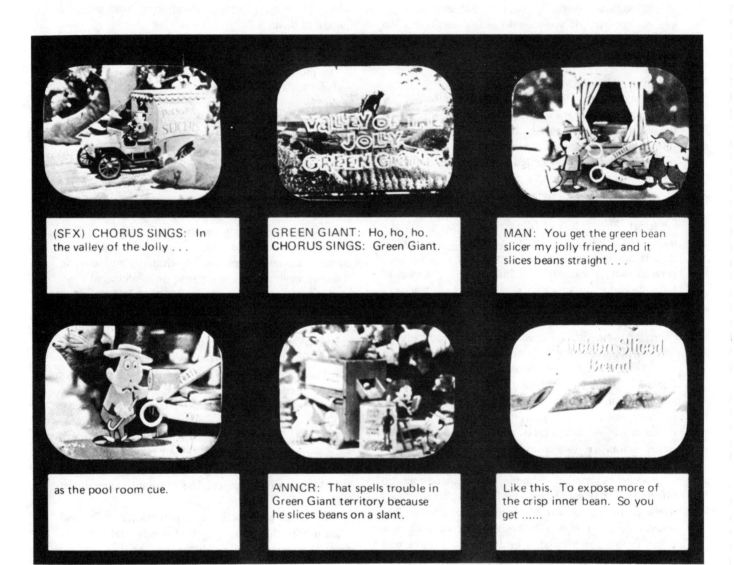

(SFX) CHORUS SINGS: In the valley of the Jolly . . .

GREEN GIANT: Ho, ho, ho.
CHORUS SINGS: Green Giant.

MAN: You get the green bean slicer my jolly friend, and it slices beans straight . . .

as the pool room cue.

ANNCR: That spells trouble in Green Giant territory because he slices beans on a slant.

Like this. To expose more of the crisp inner bean. So you get ......

CHORUS SINGS: Young beans, snapin' fresh, sliced the way they taste the best.

ANNCR: Try Kitchen Sliced Brand Diagonal Cut Green Beans.

The Green Giant also takes tender kernels of his Niblets corn and puts them up . . .

with almost no water. Then Niblets corn is vacuum packed (SFX) to stay crisp.

Only the Green Giant gives you niblets Brand corn.

CHORUS SINGS: Good things from the garden, . . .

garden, . . .

garden in the valley.

Valley of the Jolly . . . GREEN GIANT: Ho, Ho, Ho. CHORUS SINGS: Green Giant.

Exhibit 4-2. Integrating Elements: Connecticut General

Advertiser: Connecticut General Life Insurance Co.

Agency: Cunningham & Walsh, Inc.

Product: Estate planning

Title: "Sandcastle"

Format: Problem-Solution/SFX/Music

Length: 30 seconds

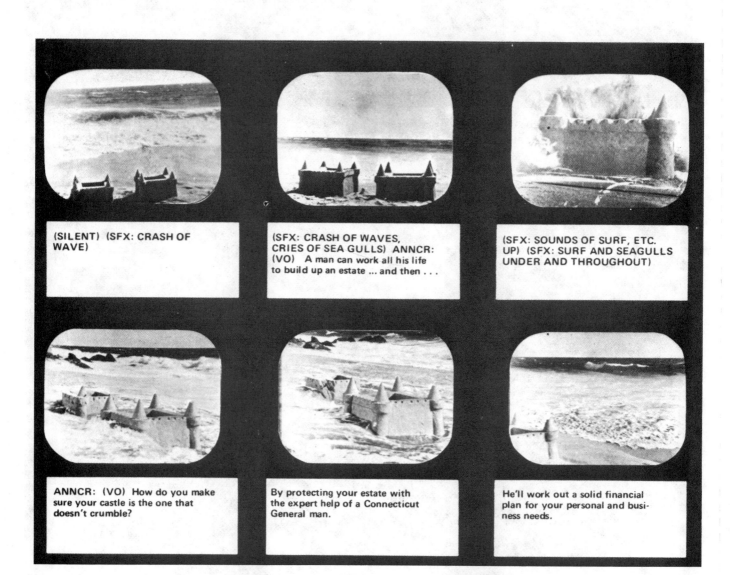

(SILENT) (SFX: CRASH OF WAVE)

(SFX: CRASH OF WAVES, CRIES OF SEA GULLS) ANNCR: (VO) A man can work all his life to build up an estate ... and then . . .

(SFX: SOUNDS OF SURF, ETC. UP) (SFX: SURF AND SEAGULLS UNDER AND THROUGHOUT)

ANNCR: (VO) How do you make sure your castle is the one that doesn't crumble?

By protecting your estate with the expert help of a Connecticut General man.

He'll work out a solid financial plan for your personal and business needs.

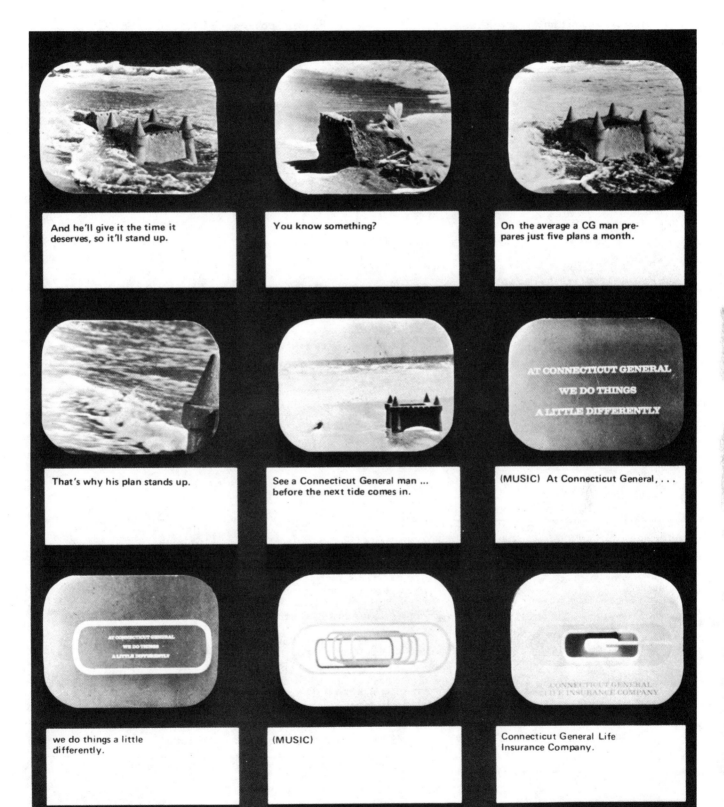

And he'll give it the time it deserves, so it'll stand up.

You know something?

On the average a CG man prepares just five plans a month.

That's why his plan stands up.

See a Connecticut General man ... before the next tide comes in.

(MUSIC) At Connecticut General, ...

we do things a little differently.

(MUSIC)

Connecticut General Life Insurance Company.

Exhibit 4-3. Integrating Elements: Mocap

Advertiser: Mobil Chemical Co.

Agency: The Martin Agency

Product: Mocap nematicide-insecticide

Title: "Insects"

Format: Spokesman/SFX

Length: 30 seconds

ANNCR:	If you could hear the insects that eat your corn, you'd start using Mocap nematicide-insecticide as soon as possible. If you could hear the rootworms...
SFX:_ _ _ _ _ _ _ _	ROARING
ANNCR:	wireworms...
SFX:_ _ _ _ _ _ _ _	SCREECHING
ANNCR:	nematodes...
SFX:_ _ _ _ _ _ _ _	HISSING
ANNCR:	and black cutworms.
SFX:_ _ _ _ _ _ _ _	CRUNCHING
ANNCR:	If you could hear the worms robbing you of forty bushels of corn or more per acre...If you could hear the cutworms cutting your good, healthy stalks off at the base...
SFX:_ _ _ _ _ _ _ _	TIMBER FALLING
ANNCR:	If only you could hear it...
SFX:_ _ _ _ _ _ _ _	SILENCE
ANNCR:	But you can't. So you may be sitting back using no insecticide at all. Hoping the worms won't do too much damage this year. Or maybe you're using an insecticide that doesn't protect against all four of these deadly pests. We repeat: If you could hear the rootworms, wireworms, nematodes, and black cutworms, you'd be using Mocap--the only insecticide in America that protects against all four. Because you're in the business to save corn. And so is Mocap. Mocap. Get it.
SFX:_ _ _ _ _ _ _ _	ROARING
ANNCR:	And save the corn.

Section Two:
Radio Commercials

In 1922, two years after the first regular radio programing began on stations KDKA in Pittsburgh and WWJ in Detroit, New York's WEAF broadcast the first radio commercial. The advertiser, a tenant-owned apartment complex in Queens, paid $40 for a 15-minute daytime program on the advantages of suburban living. Ironically, the first radio commercial was actually an "infomercial"—that is, the kind of in-depth advertisement that eventually disappeared from radio because of increasing costs and has returned to use via cable television within the last decade.

Two years later, National Carbide Co. became the first network advertiser. In 1926, Wheaties aired the first singing commercial. And in 1931, A&P broke through the almost decade-long ban on mentioning product features in radio spots. The company was permitted to tell listeners how much its products cost.

Besides the industry's periodic revision of its codes governing program content (the first was established in 1929 by the National Association of Broadcasters) and its various attempts to find a reliable way to measure the size of radio audiences (beginning in 1930), the most important developments in the medium, at least as far as advertisers are concerned, were (1) the establishment of commercial FM stations in 1941, (2) the first network purchase of radio programs in 1948 (they were originally developed and owned by advertisers and agencies), and (3) radio's recovery of its television-watching audience in the 1950s (which was aided by radical changes in programing formats).

Radio Today

In the same year in which the first radio commercial was aired, Herbert Hoover, later President of the United States and then, as Secretary of Commerce, responsible for administering the Radio Act of 1912, commented on the astonishing increase in the number of radio owners and in the size of the radio audience: "We have witnessed in the last four or five months one of the most astounding things that has come under my observation. . . . Today, over 600,000 persons possess wireless telephone receiving sets, whereas there were less than 50,000 such sets a year ago."

If he were alive today, Mr. Hoover would undoubtedly be even more astounded to know that there are almost 500 million radios in the United States and that more than 98 percent of all American homes have at least one.

In 1923, there were 573 radio stations in the country; today there are about 9,000 AM and FM stations. According to the Radio Advertising Bureau (RAB), the average U.S. household has 5.5 radios. Ninety-five percent of all cars have radios. Every year, people buy 10 million more radios. It is estimated that sets in use increased by 197 percent from 1960 and by 47 percent from 1970. Equally significant, the number of car radios in use has grown by 53 percent since 1970.

The increase in the number of special-interest stations has had a profound effect on the listening habits of the American consumer. RAB statistics indicate that radio reaches 96.5 percent of all men and 94.1 percent of all women each week. The latest Arbitron rating service listenership figures show that Americans listen to radio for three hours and 27 minutes per day and more than 22 hours per week. Advertisers know that commercial messages can be delivered to listeners no matter where they are located. Researchers have found that 60 percent of all people tune in to radio at home, 18 percent listen in cars, and 22 percent are potential customers elsewhere—at work, in stores, at the beach, in parks—and even on sidewalks.

Radio's invasion of the streets has been aided by the popularity of battery-powered sets, including both large portables and walk-along, miniature receivers equipped with earphones and used by joggers and mass transit riders. An estimated 8,000,000 walk-along sets are now in use, two-thirds of which are owned by listeners over the age of 18. Thus, far from dying when that technological wonder, television, entered the scene, radio has benefited from its own technological advances and has taken on a prosperous life of its own.

Back in the 1950s, after the first devastating impact of television had subsided, radio transformed itself. It turned to more modest programing and to many small advertisers to make up the revenue it had lost. It began to feature what had been its filler material, using news and music as its staples and seeking regional and local, rather than national, advertisers. Through foresight, flexibility, and innovation, radio revitalized itself and became a prime medium for advertisers, large and small.

Radio Advertising

Today, large cities may have 20 or more radio stations, and even small country towns usually have an AM outlet. With such localizing of audiences, retailers have taken full advantage of radio as an advertising medium. That it works can be inferred from an RAB survey showing that local retail sales doubled from the 1960s to the 1970s. In the mid-1980s, radio advertising exceeded $5 billion annually, a fivefold increase since the mid-1970s.

People listen to radio primarily for information, news, talk, entertainment, and sports. Nearly 95 percent of the population, 12 years of age or older, listen to some radio broadcasts every day. And from early morning to the start of prime evening time, more people listen to radio than watch television. Interestingly, the RAB reports that more than 50 percent of the adult population rate radio as a release from loneliness and boredom. It is a very personal medium for advertisers.

Important, too, is the fact that radio is an intimate, friendly medium. Disc jockeys, open mike hosts, and local commentators attract and hold audiences today as did the network personalities of the "golden age" of radio when "Fibber McGee and Molly," "Amos 'n' Andy," and Jack Benny were tune-in musts.

In addition, radio early established an amazing believability. Orson Welles's famous 1938 broadcast, based on H. G. Wells's *War of the Worlds,* "visualized" an invasion from Mars that frightened millions of listeners and moved thousands to flee from their homes in terror. As Mr. Welles said at a radio workshop, "Oh, we knew that radio, used inventively, could glue the listener to his overstuffed Morris chair, get him involved, and make him believe. . . . But we never dreamed to what extent."

Personal, friendly, and believable are attributes of radio that should not be ignored by anyone attempting to write effective commercials. Advertisers, large or local, wisely include radio in their marketing mix. Accounts with even modest national budgets can work wonders with radio alone. One jams and jellies company, Smucker, has used radio extensively with a unique creative approach to establish its name nationally. Most supermarket brands sold for a few cents less than Smucker's, so radio spots had to give housewives the idea of high quality. This goal was accomplished with a mildly self-deprecatory "recall trap." Every spot used this reminder: "With a name like Smucker's, it has to be good." Listeners across the country could identify this line, readily recall the brand name, and play back the quality message.

Many other advertisers have used radio extensively, if not exclusively. General Mills, which found success with heavy spot radio campaigns for Nature Valley Granola and Granola Bars, Breakfast Squares, and Golden Grahams, has boosted its radio spending from zero to more than $7,000,000. The big spenders in the medium, Anheuser-Busch and General Motors, each invested about $40,000,000 annually in the early 1980s. Delta Airlines and Stroh Brewery spent more than 25 percent of their advertising money in network radio during the same period. The reason? The medium works. Midas International, after adding radio to its usual television schedule, credited that mix with boosting sales 30 percent in one year.

It should be remembered, however, that such success is not automatic. People seldom just sit and listen to radio attentively. They are busy doing other things while their radios are turned on. More perhaps than with any other advertising medium, the basics of attention, interest, involvement, and conviction must be achieved in each radio commercial.

Radio has also made great strides in audience measurement. Gone is the idea of *homes* listening to radio, for homes don't listen. People listen. The old research technologies did not keep up with the multiplicity of radio sets around the house, in the car, and at the office. The old mechanical gadgetry underestimated radio's audience. So the industry—the Radio Advertising Bureau and the National Association of Broadcasters combined—undertook the All-Radio Methodology Study (ARMS I) to determine which methods of audience measurement might provide station owners and advertisers with an accurate determination of their listeners.

As a result, better ways of counting audiences were invented. Advertisers on radio now have a much better idea of what their dollars deliver. Along with local market studies by ARB, Pulse, Mediastat, Hooper, The Source, and others, a national measurement was developed. The national networks cooperated to create their own study to replace the old Nielsen national homes-listening research that depended on meters too large to be attached to all the sets in a household.

Advantages

Some media prophets of doom predicted radio's demise as an advertising medium when television entered the scene. They couldn't have been more wrong. Radio revenues did dip drastically, but broadcasters examined the medium for its strengths, fed and exercised them, and came up with new programing—and commercial health. Today, radio is a potent selling tool for good reasons. The five following advantages stand out.

1. *Radio is ubiquitous.* Nearly half a billion radios are in working order. Of these, 73 percent are in homes, stores, barbershops, and offices. Trucks and cars account for well over 100,000,000 of them. And portable radios by the scores of millions are toted just about everywhere—even to sporting events that are being broadcast play by play. Furthermore, unlike the print media, radio can't be ignored. If you're within

hearing range of a turned-on radio, you'll hear it—whether you want to or not.

2. *Radio is selective.* The geographic, demographic, and programing diversity of radio stations helps media buyers pinpoint their target audiences. Such flexibility means that your spots can be read by a live announcer on local stations. Or they can be broadcast on regional or national networks. They can be aired at just about any hour of the day or night. Advertisers can choose from a variety of AM or FM stations, each with a distinctive format: all news, adult contemporary, country, black, oldies, top forty, beautiful music, middle of the road (MOR), classical, talk, ethnic, or foreign language. Such diversity allows the copywriter to "speak" directly to his intended prospects.

3. *Radio is economical.* In a single week, radio reaches nine out of ten people 12 years of age and over. Those 18 and older listen for nearly three and a half hours a day. An advertiser can usually count on an effective combination of reach and frequency for a relatively low cost per thousand listeners. Alone or in a mix with other media, radio can effectively help stretch ad budgets. Spots can be scheduled for as few or as many plays as objectives and budget dictate.

Another economy: Radio commercials are relatively inexpensive to produce, ranging from no cost, when a script or ad-lib fact sheet is used by a live/local announcer, to a modestly budgeted full production with music, sound effects, and talent.

4. *Radio is fast.* If the need arises, an advertiser can have a live/local commercial on the air within hours. Spots using sound effects, music or jingle, and several voices can be rehearsed, recorded, mixed, dubbed, and then played on the air within days. This is a break for advertisers who must meet occasional emergencies, such as an air-conditioner dealer whose territory is suddenly smothered by a heat wave.

5. *Radio is participatory.* Along with a sense of friendliness and loyalty to a particular station, listeners develop a sense of involvement. Radio calls the imagination into play. Commercial "stories" are unrestricted as to place or time. Sound effects and music instantly establish a scene. Description or dialogue can be as vivid as taste allows, and characters can be played either straight or as comic caricatures. The listener fills in the "color" and details with his imagination.

Any or all of these characteristics of radio can be used to advantage by creative advertisers and agencies to prepare and present commercials that sell.

Guidelines

The following list of do's and don't's has been distilled from a review of the successes and failures in radio advertising over the last three decades. Consider these suggestions in deciding what will work best for your radio spot.

1. *Write for the ear.* Write conversationally. Forget that there may be thousands of people listening to your message. Write as if you are talking to one person. And be sure to make your commercial *visually* and *conceptually* clear through words and sounds.

2. *Capture and excite the listener's imagination.* By using only sound, your spot must perform effectively in the "theater of the mind." With the competition your product (and your commercial) faces, you can't afford to be dull, pedantic, or prosaic.

3. *Stick to one strong idea.* Concentrate on one main persuasive thrust. You can add an extra copy point or two, but do it with care. Too many messages confuse. Also, don't sell generically for the whole product category; sell *your* product's benefits.

4. *Single out your prospect.* If you've done your research, you know who buys your product and why. Keep your target consumer in mind when you write your commercial. If your product alleviates backache, don't start by describing June roses. Get right to the point—"If you suffer the agony of a sore back. . . ." Your talent selection can help. A company making skin care products featured a nationally famous disc jockey talking to teenagers about acne. Because of his involvement with popular music, he was a listened-to authority figure, and he successfully reached the intended audience.

5. *Set the mood for your product.* How fast should your commercial be delivered? What tone of voice should your "housewife" employ? Is the music too "busy" for your product's image? These and a dozen other questions should come to mind when you write a commercial. Your answers will determine the "tone" or approach. To get the right one, you must be conscious of *how* you want the listener to hear—and react.

After deciding on tone, write directions in your script as to how you wish each line to be read ("angry," "happy," "sad," "irritated," etc.). A spokesperson picking up your script should have specific directions. When you indicate the kind of delivery you want, everyone—from the client to the director—benefits.

It's worth repeating: Radio can do just about anything, from a straightforward, news-oriented sales pitch to a wildly imaginative satire. But you must be careful not to get carried away. The commercial's tone should match the product's image; they should be compatible.

6. *Remember your mnemonics.* Be sure to set a memory trap—and spring it. It might be in the copy, the music, the sound effects, or a combination thereof, but it must be meaningful. If you can use a distinctive and memorable sound—the "hummmmmmm" of a Mazda engine or the "Mm-mm good!" response of a child eating Campbell's soup—use it.

Diet Pepsi zipped up a zipper, Alka-Seltzer plopped and fizzed, and Park sausages had an insistent boy's voice pleading, "More Park sausages, please."

7. *Get attention fast.* The first five or six seconds in a radio commercial are vitally important. If you fail here, the whole spot may be a wasted effort. An auto-

motive product began a commercial with an announcer speaking over a public-address system at a race course: "Gentlemen, start your engines!" And immediately afterward a roar of engines was heard. Expend a lot of creative thought on your opening.

8. *Register the product's name.* Some copy chiefs might add, "Early and often!" Since you don't have the use of headlines, as you do in print advertising, or even a shot of the actual product, as in television, you must establish the product name by repeating it during the spot.

One commercial for Triumph cars began with a local announcer giving a dealer's name and address, followed by "Your Triumph dealer takes you out on the range." The pretaped spot included the sound of a horse neighing and a Triumph driving up and stopping. A cowboy drawled, "See you hitched up to a Triumph, Slim."

In this case, the listener couldn't help but identify the product name—and quickly. You can also spell out the name, as Sanka decaffeinated coffee did in the 1940s, with each letter punctuated by the sound of a gun blast supposedly shot by fictional detective Sam Spade. Or you can pun on the product's name if it is also a word with favorable connotations, such as United, True Value, or Brim.

9. *Don't overwrite.* Don't crowd your spot with too much copy. Like "white space" in print ads, silence (for at least a second or two) can help focus attention on your main message. Use easy-to-understand words, and keep phrases and sentences on the short side. Write in the present tense and active voice as much as possible.

Read your commercial aloud or have someone read it to you. Change any words that interrupt continuity or are difficult to pronounce. Allow for announcer breathing (and listener hearing) time. Word count varies with approach, delivery, mood, etc., but the following figures are generally accepted averages for straight announcements.

> 10 seconds: 20– 25 words
> 20 seconds: 40– 45 words
> 30 seconds: 60– 70 words
> 60 seconds: 150– 180 words

If you find your copy running beyond these limits, make sure that it can be read within the allotted time— or rewrite it.

10. *Make your appeal clear.* There are few basic human needs (shelter, food, clothing, and love), but human wants seem unlimited. So you have a wide choice when it comes to selecting and crafting a persuasive appeal. A good question to ask is: "What want or need does this product satisfy?"

You can use logic if your product is a hard-nosed performer and you can explain why it works so well. If it saves either time or money, you should say so. But don't stop there. Go beyond cold logic into the warmer currents of emotional persuasion. Time saved can be-

come extra time for your consumer to do other things, and money saved can be spent for other fulfillments.

11. *If it's news, make it sound important.* First make sure that what you have to say *is* news. Too many commercials promising news have made customers wary. So if you're writing about the semiannual white sale at the local department store, don't treat it as an earth-shaking event. Don't make it sound as important as landing on Mars.

However, if the facts *are* important, repeat them again and again. Treat significantly lower prices, genuinely new products, and spectacular promotions the way they deserve to be treated—with the radio equivalent of big headlines and exclamatory copy.

12. *Multiply your TV impressions.* If the audio track for your television spot can double—that is, serve as a radio commercial as well—it stretches the ad dollar nicely. When a listener hears a spot he has seen on TV, it can be instantly visualized, at no extra cost to the advertiser.

Charlie the Tuna is so familiar on television that a radio spot with sound effects, music, and Charlie's familiar voice can give a mental impression of Charlie trying to be chosen by Star-Kist for his "good taste."

13. *Keep a friendly feeling going.* Engage your audience, but don't irritate or anger. Remember, you're trying to win friends, as well as influence prospective customers and retain present buyers. How many grumpy salespeople are successful? And the point applies to the entire commercial, not just the lead-in. Make it smile!

14. *Be sure that your humorous spots are funny.* Why does almost every copywriter begin by thinking that the way to sell is to be very, very funny? Not every product is amenable to humorous treatment. And not every listener has a similar sense of humor. For these reasons, many ostensibly funny commercials don't sell. Worse yet, many that seem amusing to copywriters may not be so perceived by clients and audiences.

15. *Give the reader something to do.* The bid for action, usually near the end of the commercial, is like a salesman's request for an order. What do you want the listener to do? Where? When? If it's a local spot, use an address and ask listeners to drop in. Immediate action demands a phone number. If the commercial is national, close with your strong selling theme. This gives the listener a final opportunity to react to—and commit to memory—your main appeal.

16. *Once is not enough.* If you mention a telephone number, be sure to repeat it. Keep in mind that the listener is not glued to the radio, breathlessly awaiting your sales pitch. Chances are, he or she will not have pencil and pad at the ready. Give everyone a chance to record essential information, including address and even store hours. Your spot may be spectacular, but if customers don't know where to go or whom to call in order to get the product, you've lost sales and wasted your valuable time.

Examples 6

National Radio Commercials

The commercials on the following pages were originally aired on network radio. In most cases, they have been selected as good examples of radio advertising because they were successful. In fact, some of the spots actually helped to reverse a decline in sales, and a few turned a big loss into a comfortable profit.

Some of the formats discussed in Chapter 3 are represented by one or two commercials. Several of the spots use sound effects, dialogue, and/or music. Pay special attention to the way in which these elements are integrated. Note how different elements are used with different formats and different products. Although the commercials shown here differ in format, style, and technique—as well as marketing objective and target audience—they are all attention-getting and persuasive.

For each spot, we have provided the names of the advertiser, the agency (when available), and the product or service; the type of format; and the length. A brief analysis, emphasizing special appeals and unusual elements, follows each radio script.

Formal radio scripts are usually laid out in a special way. The left side of the page, typed in capital letters, indicates who is speaking and whether and when music and sound effects (SFX) are to be used. The right side, typed in both upper and lower case letters, presents all the copy that is to be read. In addition, special instructions and directions concerning music and sound effects are given in caps. Sound effects are underlined with a broken line. Music directions are underlined with a solid line.

Exhibit 6-1. Slice of Life: Blue Nun

Advertiser: Schieffelin & Co. Title: "Cruise"

Agency: Cunningham & Walsh Inc. Format: Slice of Life

Product: Blue Nun wine Length: 60 seconds

Script

STILLER: Excuse me, the cruise director assigned me this table for dinner.

MEARA: Say, weren't you the fella at the costume ball last night dressed as a giant tuna? With scales, the gills, and the fins?

STILLER: Yeah--that was me.

MEARA: I recognized you right away.

STILLER: Were you there?

MEARA: I was dressed as a mermaid so I had to spend most of the night sitting down. Did you ever try dancing with both legs wrapped in aluminum foil?

STILLER: No, I can't say I have. Did you order dinner yet?

MEARA: I'm having the filet of sole.

STILLER: Hmmm. The filet mignon looks good. Would you like to share a bottle of wine?

MEARA: Terrific.

STILLER: I noticed a little Blue Nun at the Captain's table.

MEARA: Poor thing. Maybe she's seasick.

STILLER: No, Blue Nun is a wine. A delicious white wine.

MEARA: Oh, we can't have a white wine if you're having meat and I'm having fish.

STILLER: Sure we can. Blue Nun is a white wine that's correct with any dish. Your filet of sole. My filet mignon.

MEARA:	Oh, it's so nice to meet a man who knows the finer things. You must be a gourmet.
STILLER:	No, as a matter of fact, I'm an accountant. Small firm in the city. Do a lot of tax work...
ANNCR:	Blue Nun. The delicious white wine that's correct with any dish. Another Sichel wine imported by Schieffelin & Co., New York.

Analysis

This slice-of-life example uses the unique humor of established actors in a recognizable situation to introduce the product. It follows the advertising strategy (Blue Nun is the one wine that is correct with any dish) and combines a persuasive reminder with entertainment. What gives this spot uniqueness? The comedic talents of Gerry Stiller and Anne Meara, who underplay, speak in natural, conversational tones, and deliver their lines with perfect timing. The main idea comes through clearly, and the commercial is a delight to listen to again and again.

Exhibit 6-2. Spokesman: True Value

Advertiser: Cotter & Co.

Agency: Christenson, Barclay & Shaw, Inc.

Product: Sunbeam Hotshot

Title: "Christmas/Hotshot"

Format: Spokesman

Length: 60 seconds

Script

ANNCR: True Value Hardware Stores suggest you give a Christmas gift that <u>really</u> makes instant coffee, soup, or cocoa. Give the Sunbeam Hotshot.

Hi, I'm ANNOUNCER'NAME to tell you that you're not really making instant coffee, soup, or cocoa if you take the time to boil water in a pot. When you use the Sunbeam Hotshot, you get about 12 ounces of hot water in only about 90 seconds with the touch of a lever. That's <u>really</u> instant coffee! Plus, it's really convenient when you only want to make one or two cups of the hot beverage. You'll find the Sunbeam Hotshot at participating True Value Hardware Stores. And you'll recognize it by its compact size, with a cord that stores in the back, and by its attractive Harvest Gold exterior with a rich wood-tone finish front.

So, if you want to give a Christmas gift that <u>really</u> makes instant hot beverages, get the Sunbeam Hotshot. Because you're not really making instant coffee if you take the time to boil water in a pot. You'll find it at participating True Value Hardware Stores. Tell 'em ANNOUNCER'S NAME sent you.

Analysis

This example shows that the oldest radio format can still be among the most effective. It is easy to listen to. It is hard-hitting. It tells the product name, indicates what it does, and gives a personal reason to buy—all in the first 22 words. No music, no sound effects, but plenty of well-crafted identification copy for store and appliance, some quick demonstration copy, and good use of repetition. True Value adds to the listenability of its spots by using well-known broadcast personalities.

Exhibit 6-3. Testimonial: Cold Power

Advertiser: Colgate-Palmolive Co.

Agency: Norman, Craig & Kummel

Product: Cold Power detergent

Title: "Energy Saver"

Format: Testimonial

Length: 30 seconds

Script

SFX:_ _ _ _ _ _ _ _ TELEPHONE DIALING, RINGING SOUND

ALLAN ROBERTS: What's your secret for saving energy? We called Mrs. Ruby LeBlanc of New Orleans to find out hers. Hi, this is Allan Roberts. Are you doing anything to save energy in your home?

MRS. LEBLANC: I put insulation in my attic.

ALLAN ROBERTS: Anything else?

MRS. LEBLANC: I'm using cold water. Your clothes stay nicer, and then you're not using energy with the hot water.

ALLAN ROBERTS: What laundry detergent do you use?

MRS. LEBLANC: Cold Power. It's specially made to work in cold water.

ALLAN ROBERTS: And up to 20% of your fuel bill goes to heating water.

MRS. LEBLANC: I think we ought to save energy for the children.

ALLAN ROBERTS: How many do you have?

MRS. LEBLANC: Just one. She fools with automobiles. She gets greasy. Cold Power gets my clothes beautiful and I save energy.

ALLAN ROBERTS: Try the cold water cleaning specialist. Cold Power XE.

Analysis

Dialogue is extremely difficult to do well. Too often, it sounds stilted and artificial. In this detergent commercial, however, it is handled expertly, and the product benefit comes across subtly and painlessly. Note that the testimonial is offered by a stock character, the "typical" housewife, in a stock situation, an interview.

Exhibit 6-4. Musical: Michelob

Advertiser: Anheuser-Busch Cos.

Agency: D'Arcy-MacManus & Masius

Product: Michelob beer

Title: "Duet"

Format: Musical

Length: 60 seconds

Script

FEMALE:	MICHELOB
MALE:	SOME THINGS SPEAK FOR THEMSELVES
FEMALE:	MICHELOB
MALE:	SMOOTH
FEMALE:	SMOOTH AND MELLOW
MALE:	MICHELOB
FEMALE:	SOME THING SPECIAL
TOGETHER:	MICHELOB. SOME THINGS SPEAK FOR THEMSELVES.
MALE:	JUST ONE TASTE
FEMALE:	TELLS YOU ALL
MALE:	MICHELOB
FEMALE:	ALL YOU NEED TO KNOW
CHORUS:	MICHELOB
FEMALE:	MICHELOB
MALE:	SOME THINGS SPEAK FOR THEMSELVES
FEMALE:	MICHELOB
TOGETHER:	SOME THINGS SPEAK FOR THEMSELVES
MALE:	Anheuser-Busch, St. Louis, Missouri

Analysis

This effective radio spot supplemented a television campaign. Unlike the AT&T and Dr Pepper commercials (Exhibits 6-5 and 6-6), however, the Michelob TV version showed the product alone—with musical accompaniment. Using a nonvisual medium, the copywriter concentrated on the music. Note that the theme is repeated four times; the product name, eight times. Note also that the music is not up-tempo and "jingly." Like its TV counterpart, it creates a "mellow" mood suggestive of the quieter pleasures of beer drinking.

Exhibit 6-5. Musical: AT&T

Advertiser: AT&T Communications   Title: "Charlie Pride"

Agency: N W Ayer   Format: Musical

Product: Long-distance telephone calling   Length: 45 seconds

---

Script

VO: AT&T presents Charlie Pride for long distance.

CHARLIE: GRANDPA'S PLAYIN A TUNE ON THE FIDDLE

             AND THE TWINS ARE GETTIN TALL

             UNCLE JOE GOT BIG AROUND THE MIDDLE

             AND SUE'S GETTIN MARRIED IN THE FALL

             GRANNY JUST STARTED DANCIN WITH THE PREACHER

             EVERYONE'S HAVIN A BALL

             WE KNEW YOU COULDN'T MAKE IT HOME FOR THE PARTY

             SO WE FIGURED WE'D GIVE YOU A CALL

             REACH OUT, REACH OUT AND TOUCH SOMEONE

             REACH OUT, CALL UP AND JUST SAY HI

VO: The folks who miss the party don't have to miss

             the fun. Bring the party to them with a long

             distance call.

             EVERYONE HERE IS ASKIN FOR YOU

             WISH YOU COULD OF COME BACK HOME

             BUT THE NEXT BEST THING TO HAVING YOU AROUND

             IS HEARIN YOU ON THE PHONE

             REACH OUT, REACH OUT AND TOUCH SOMEONE

VO: When a faraway voice sounds as close as you feel,

             that's reach out and touch someone.

             That's AT&T.

Analysis

Sometimes the entire selling message can be conveyed in words and music. In this instance, it was done exceptionally well, and the theme "Reach out and touch someone" actually gained emotional impact from the musical rendition. A strong TV campaign, run simultaneously, gave the radio version instant "visual" impact. Anyone who had seen the television spot automatically imagined the video portion.

Exhibit 6-6. Musical: Dr Pepper

Advertiser: Dr Pepper Co.

Agency: Young & Rubicam

Product: Dr Pepper soft drink

Title: "David Naughton"

Format: Musical

Length: 30 seconds

Script

ANNCR: For Dr Pepper, here's David Naughton.

VOCAL: I DRINK DR PEPPER, DON'T YOU SEE,

'CAUSE IT'S A PERFECT TASTE FOR ME.

THAT ORIGINAL TASTE, YOU KNOW,

IS MAKIN' PEPPERS EVERYWHERE YOU GO.

EVERYWHERE YOU GO ARE PEPPERS,

LOTS OF FOLKS YOU KNOW ARE PEPPERS,

WOULDN'T YOU LIKE TO BE A PEPPER, TOO?

I'M A PEPPER, HE'S A PEPPER,

SHE'S A PEPPER, YOU'RE A PEPPER,

WE'RE A PEPPER...

EVERYWHERE YOU GO ARE PEPPERS,

WOULDN'T YOU LIKE TO BE A PEPPER, TOO?

I'M A PEPPER, HE'S A PEPPER,

WE'RE A PEPPER...

DRINK DR PEPPER, TOO!

Analysis

This commercial is based on the somewhat silly-sounding phrase "Be a Pepper." It may not make much sense, but it worked, particularly as presented here in a frenetically fast-paced delivery of the lyrics, which make the product sound lively and refreshing. Like the AT&T spot, this one created a "visual" accompaniment because it was aired in conjunction with a TV commercial using the same song and talent. David Naughton, the "star" of a series of Dr Pepper musicals, was relatively unknown before his appearance in this company's long-running campaign.

Exhibit 6-7. Testimonial/Musical: Red Lobster

Advertiser: Red Lobster Inns

Agency: D'Arcy-MacManus & Masius

Product: Spiced shrimp dinner

Title: "AM Drive Time/Shrimp"

Formats: Testimonial/Musical

Length: 60 seconds

Script:

SINGERS:	HOW DO YOU LIKE YOUR SHRIMP,
	WE KNOW HOW YOU LIKE YOUR SHRIMP!
	RED LOBSTER FOR THE SEAFOOD ...
JOEL:	And shrimp!
SINGERS:	LOVER IN YOU!
JOEL:	You know, usually I don't make my dinner plans while I'm driving to work in the morning ... but one has to be flexible ... and the idea of sitting down to a half pound of spiced shrimp at Red Lobster tonight, well it sounds delicious. Think of it ... a half pound of shrimp cooked up in a spicy blend of seasonings ... you just peel 'em, pop 'em in your mouth and Ahhhhh. Ready for another one? There you go, ohhhh ... hot ... hot. How 'bout a shrimp dinner at Red Lobster tonight? Be strong now ... wait till dinner ... ah about eight hours from now ... oh make that seven hours fifty nine minutes & 12 seconds ... You can do it....
SINGERS:	HOW DO YOU LIKE YOUR SHRIMP,
	WE KNOW HOW YOU LIKE YOUR SHRIMP,
	RED LOBSTER FOR THE SEAFOOD ...
JOEL:	It'll give you something to look forward to!
SINGERS:	LOVER IN YOU!
RECORDED TAG:	Spiced Shrimp are something deliciously new at Red Lobster. Come in and try 'em tonight!

Analysis

The Red Lobster jingle, made familiar to both radio and TV audiences by frequent repetition, served as a readily identifiable company signature. Although the jingle remained the same in every commercial, each spot in the continuing series featured a different Red Lobster specialty. Note that the testifier is cast in the role of his audience, people driving to work. And his appeal is directly, dramatically, to the senses.

Exhibit 6-8. Spokesman/Slice of Life/Musical: WICO

Advertiser: WICO Corp.

Agency: Bentley, Barnes & Lynn, Inc.

Product: WICO joysticks

Title: "Whacko over WICO"

Formats: Spokesman/Slice of life/Musical

Length: 60 seconds

Script

SONG: YOUR STICKO WON'T GO WHACKO WHEN IT'S A WICO.
(REPEAT)

ANNCR: WICO won't go whacko because it's the only authentic arcade joystick you can use at home. Over 500 arcade video games use WICO controls. The most durable, the most accurate ... the fastest controls money can buy.

BOY: Wow! I'm scoring at home like I've never scored. I'm whacko over WICO.

SONG: YOUR STICKO WON'T GO WHACKO WHEN IT'S A WICO.

TEEN BOY: They're as tough as the joysticks at the arcade.

TEEN GIRL: He's whacko over WICO.

MOM: I've been practicing.

DAD: She's whacko over WICO.

ANNCR: There are more WICO joysticks than you can shake a stick at. Command Control Joysticks, Computer Control Joysticks, and the new BOSS that lets you boss any game around.

SONG: YOUR STICKO WON'T GO WHACKO WHEN IT'S A WICO.
(REPEAT)

Analysis

This radio spot, which complemented the television commercial shown in Exhibit 3-2, similarly combines different formats. The memorable jingle frames the sketch. The spokesman, providing specific product information, speaks after the opening and before the closing song. And, in between, three members of the family convey their enthusiasm for the product, while two others give added punch to the testimony.

Local Radio Commercials

The local spots on the following pages should be regarded as outstanding work created under extreme pressure. In many cases, they are the products of copywriters constrained by severe limitations in time and money. Note that many use no music, special effects, or other production extras. The reason, of course, is that most local spots are done on a small budget, and many are written against a tight deadline. Nevertheless, like the national radio commercials shown on the preceding pages, these spots succeeded.

One further result of the budget/deadline crunch is the fact that most local commercials are straight announcements. That is, they use the spokesman format. For this reason, the following examples should be analyzed in terms of how they present product features and benefits. Some local radio spots confine themselves to only one feature or benefit. However, most emphasize more, including—most often—price, quality, variety, and convenience.

When you examine these commercials, note whether they are delivered in first (we), second (you), or third person (they). Also note sentence length, word choice, and use of sentence fragments. Do they close with an express or implied bid for action? Do they register the store or product name? For each spot, try to imagine what kind of voice and delivery would work best.

Because we have deleted the names of the advertisers in some of the announcement commercials, we have indicated only the type of retailer or dealer and the length of the spot. Again, however, an analysis follows each script.

Exhibit 6-9. Local Spot: Rheingold

Advertiser: C. Schmidt & Sons, Inc.

Agency: John Emmerling

Product: Rheingold beer

Title: "Supermarket"

Format: Slice of Life

Length: 60 seconds

Script

MUSIC:	STOCK--STRIDENT, PATRIOTIC
ANNCR:	New York is learning that Rheingold ... the extra dry beer with a stout, creamy head that stands up longer than Schaefer, Miller, and even the expensive import Heineken ... that Rheingold is now out to beat inflation. Here now, a typical checkout counter ...
MUSIC/SFX:	MUSIC FADES INTO BABBLE OF SUPERMARKET SOUNDS
WOMAN CHECKER (CHEWING GUM):	Asparagus ...
SFX:	CASH REGISTER SOUND
CHECKER:	$3.29 ... Chuck roast
SFX:	CASH REGISTER SOUND
CHECKER:	$6.50 ... Rheingold beer ... Wait a minute! This price is marked wrong! It's too low!
MAN:	Yeah, listen ... I'm in a hurry. I just want to ...
CHECKER:	Hold on, honey! Beer prices are up all over town...
MAN (QUIETLY FURTIVE):	Well, maybe you could let the Rheingold slip through this time ...
CHECKER (BECOMING INDIGNANT):	This is America, fella! Raising prices is practically patriotic! Manager! Manager to checkout six!
MANAGER (DEEP VOICE):	Okay, what's the trouble here?

MAN:	Well, nothing really ...
CHECKER:	This guy is trying to buy Rheingold at the wrong price.
MANAGER:	Frieda, Rheingold is out to beat inflation. That's the right price.
CHECKER (TO HERSELF):	That's the right price? (TO CUSTOMER) Oh, sir, I owe you an apology ...
MAN:	Yeah ... I'll settle for the beer.
MUSIC:	STRIDENT, PATRIOTIC THEME
ANNCR:	And so, fellow New Yorkers, check the price of the beer you drink--then check Rheingold. Try the premium quality that beats inflation. Rheingold!

Analysis

It's not easy to combine music, sound effects, humor, and dialogue into an effective and comprehensible commercial. This one does it so forcefully that it actually turned sales around in a matter of weeks. Although this spot deals with a problem (inflation) and a solution (inexpensive beer), it does not follow the problem-solution format. The slice-of-life scene takes place in a supermarket and is played out by three ''average'' characters.

Exhibit 6-10. Local Spot: Magee's

Advertiser: Magee's Clothing

Agency: Ayres & Associates, Inc.

Product: Jeans

Title: "Jeans, Not Rock"

Formats: Slice of life/Musical

Length: 60 seconds

Script

MUSIC:	ESTABLISH LIGHT ROCK RHYTHM, KEEP UNDER DIALOGUE
MAN:	Hey, Magee's Stone Woman, you still making history?
WOMAN:	I sure hope not.
MAN:	Listen, Stone Lady, we're worried about your super-cool costume. The winters here are very whippy, and we think your little dinosaur dress is going to give you leg cramps. How about if we turn your teeny dress into a top and put it over some new jeans from Magee's Junior Girls?
WOMAN:	You trying to change my style?
MAN:	Now don't be paranoid.
WOMAN:	Para ... what?
MAN:	Paranoid. Means clever as a chicken. Many of Magee's new jeans have a gold underwear stitch around the powderhorn pockets and down the side ...
WOMAN:	Talk rock!
MAN:	Can't. I don't know how. Some have buttons, some zip fronts, some high-rise, some wide waistbands, some wide legs ...
WOMAN:	Talk rock!
MAN:	I can't, Stone Woman. I don't understand your crazy rock talk. Now, many of Magee's junior-girl jeans are by Prophet and Friends ...
WOMAN:	... rock music!

MAN:	Nah, the Prophet and Friends group makes <u>jeans</u>,
	not music ... course, you could wear 'em to rock
	around the campfire on cold nights ...
WOMAN:	Aha! <u>That's</u> rock talk. Your cave or mine?
JINGLE:	HEY, WHEN YOU WANNA BE WHAT YOU WANNA BE,
	WHY DON'T YOU COME AND SEE MAGEE'S.
	SEE MAGEE'S, LINCOLN AND OMAHA,
	SEE MAGEE'S.
MUSIC:	END

Analysis

Notice how this commercial reaches for its special audience—junior girls—with an imaginary Stone Age character. One of a continuing series, this spot gets to the product easily and quickly, then uses the time-honored technique of dialogue in which one character doesn't seem to understand what the other (who usually gives the sales pitch) is talking about. This technique keeps the subject alive and developing and the copy points coming until the final fillip. The jingle serves as a strong reminder as well as a bid for action.

Exhibit 6-11. Local Spot: French Creek

Advertiser: French Creek Sheep & Wool Co.

Product: Sheepskin coats

Format: Spokesman

Length: 60 seconds

Script

SFX:_ _ _ _ _ _ _ _ GENERAL OUTDOOR RANCH SOUNDS: RUSTLE OF LEAVES,_
TWITTERING OF BIRDS, BLEATING OF SHEEP, BARK OF _
SHEEPDOG. ESTABLISH 4 SECONDS, THEN DOWN AND_
UNDER VOICE THROUGHOUT.

ERIC FLAXENBURG: One of the most beautiful sights that spring has
to offer is a flock of sheep pasturing on a rolling
green hillside. I'm Eric Flaxenburg, and I ought
to know. Along with my wife, Jean, I own and
operate a small Chester County Sheep Ranch...the
French Creek Sheep & Wool Company...where some of
the very finest sheepskin coats in the world are
made. Handcrafted in the French Creek tradition by
people who really love their work. Evidently, most
of our regular listeners agree, because the
response to our annual sale of sheepskin coats has
been nothing short of phenomenal. But we're still
hearing from friends who haven't been able to get
out to see us yet, so Jean and I have decided to
extend the sale just a little longer. To give
them...and you...the chance to save 20 percent on
handsome sheepskin coats and jackets for men and
women. We'll even custom make you a coat at 10
percent savings if you can't find your coat in
stock. Since the price of pelts will probably rise
again this fall, this is the perfect chance for
you to save substantially on the sheepskin coat

you've always wanted to own...at French Creek

Sheep & Wool Company. For directions and

additional information, call 1-286-5700. That's

1-286-5700.

Analysis

Here is information plus persuasion. The mood and stage are set with the sound effects. They "take" the listener into the country in the first few seconds. The company co-owner, Eric Flaxenburg, speaks in a friendly, well-modulated but conversational voice—as if he were talking with someone he knew quite well. The dialogue is not rushed, and each point seems to follow easily from the preceding point. There is an urgency in the possible price rise and good help in the closing bid for action.

Exhibit 6-12. Local Spot: Garvey's

Advertiser: Garvey's Transmission	Format: Spokesman
Service: Transmission repairs	Length: 30 seconds

Script

Analysis

Without sound effects, this commercial would be boring. With exaggerated sound-effect interruptions, however, which maintain continuity and emphasize service points, the spot keeps interest high. At the same time, it allows frequent mention of the advertiser's name and business. Voice and sound effects work together to aid recall.

ANNCR: This man is in a big hurry.

SFX:_ _ _ _ _ _ _ _WHOOSH OF JET_

ANNCR: He's headed for Garvey's Transmission, at Pike

                          and 28th.

SFX:_ _ _ _ _ _ _ _HORSE GALLOPING_

ANNCR: He arrives at Garvey's Transmission.

SFX:_ _ _ _ _ _ _ _SCREECHING BRAKES_

ANNCR: He goes into Garvey's Transmission.

SFX:_ _ _ _ _ _ _ _WOOD AND GLASS BREAKING_

ANNCR: He talks to the manager at Garvey's Transmission.

SFX:_ _ _ _ _ _ _ _SPEEDED-UP VOICES_

ANNCR: Now, he doesn't have to worry about laying out a

                          lot of cash or even a down payment at Garvey's

                          Transmission for any motor or transmission work.

SFX:_ _ _ _ _ _ _ _CASH REGISTER_

ANNCR: He gets instant credit and easy budget terms

                          with no money down, just like ...

SFX:_ _ _ _ _ _ _ _FINGERS SNAP

ANNCR: ... that! When he brought in his car, his

                         transmission ...

SFX:_ _ _ _ _ _ _ _ _ _A GRINDING "CLUNKER"

ANNCR: ... sounded like a cement mixer in reverse. And

                         in only a couple of days ...

SFX:_ _ _ _ _ _ _ _ _ _TICKING OF CLOCK

ANNCR: ... his car will ...

SFX:_ _ _ _ _ _ _ _ _ _PURRING CAT_

ANNCR: He became a happy man ...

SFX:_ _ _ _ _ _ _ _ _ _LAUGHTER

ANNCR: ... at Garvey's Transmission. And you will, too!

Exhibit 6-13. Local Spot: Restaurant

Advertiser: Restaurant   Length: 60 seconds

Script

ANNOUNCER:

You don't have to spend a fortune to take the family out to eat. Take them to (ADVERTISER), where even today you get great food at very affordable prices. At (ADVERTISER), the menu features real Italian specialties, from spaghetti and sausages to baked manicotti with veal cutlets. Then there's fried and broiled ocean-fresh seafood, a great selection of meats and chicken, plus fourteen varieties of pizza. To add to your dining pleasure, (ADVERTISER) has a fine selection of spirits, wines, and beers. From appetizers to desserts, everything is carefully prepared at (ADVERTISER). And the portions are very generous. For those who like to dine at home, (ADVERTISER) Deli take-out service is the answer. Just give them a call. Everything will be ready when you stop in to pick it up--or drop in and make your selection. It will only take a few minutes. (ADVERTISER), one of the city's oldest and finest restaurants, (LOCATION). They make dining out very affordable.

Analysis

This spot opens and closes with its main selling theme—low prices. However, it also stresses wide selection, ample servings, take-out convenience, and high quality: ''one of the city's oldest and finest restaurants.'' The advertiser's name is mentioned no less than six times in this 60-second spot. The target market is middle-income people looking for something between fast-food restaurants and expensive eateries.

Exhibit 6-14. Local Spot: Drug Store

Advertiser: Drug store   Length: 60 seconds

Script

ANNOUNCER: Some people like today's fast-paced, high-tech

modern world ... while others yearn for the good

old days, when life went by a little slower, and

you put up your feet once in a while, and just

collected your thoughts. At (ADVERTISER), we've

combined the best of both worlds....We've got

highly trained, experienced, professional phar-

macists who give your prescriptions priority and

fill them rapidly and accurately....At the same

time, we believe in our tradition of friendly,

personal service....We're glad to take the time

to show you our fine selection of vitamins and

over-the-counter remedies....We're modern and

computerized, and that's good. But we're proud,

too, that we don't just check you out and rush

you out the door. At (ADVERTISER), take as long

as you like to select the best for you and your

family. At (ADVERTISER), we've combined the old

and the new. (ADVERTISER), at (LOCATION). Open

seven days a week.

Analysis

Appeals to nostalgia are pointless unless they attach a benefit to the retreat into the past. Here, ''the good old days'' are associated with personal service. However, this drug store is not just old fashioned. It offers ''the best of both worlds''—trained personnel, modern technology, and fast, as well as attentive, service. Note that the store name is given three times in the last 30 words.

Assignments 7

The assignments in this chapter are intended to give you an opportunity to show what you have learned about radio advertising. Before you begin to write, however, review the advice about writing commercials in Chapter 2, the discussion of formats and other elements in Chapters 3 and 4, and the guidelines for writing radio spots in Chapter 5. Be sure to give yourself enough time to *think*. And choose the components of your commercial with the product, consumer, and competition in mind. If you get stuck, review the sample radio scripts in Chapter 6 for ideas and alternatives.

Some of the assignments on the following pages ask you to work with background data or with a brief summary of marketing objectives. In some instances, you will be requested to rewrite a radio, TV, or print ad—without benefit of product or market information other than what appears in the ad. In all cases, you should prepare a creative strategy statement (see Exhibits 1-1 and 1-2) based on the data available. Don't contradict the ''facts'' as they are given, but feel free to fill in the blanks when necessary. After you have written a strategy statement, study it carefully. Use it as a point of departure and keep checking it as you write to make certain that you are staying on target.

Unless your instructor tells you to do otherwise, follow the script style shown in Exhibits 6-1–6-10. That is, for every assignment, name the advertiser, indicate which format(s) you are using, name the product or service, and give the length of the commercial. In writing the script, use upper-case letters for titles or names of speakers, sound effects, music cues and copy, and stage directions. Type (double-space) all assignments.

RADIO SCRIPT SHEET

Student name: Advertiser:

Date submitted: Product:

Commercial length: Format:

Assignment 7-1: Background Data

THE CLIENT: Pet Paradise

THE PRODUCT: A full line of pet foods (seeds and pellets) for birds and small animals (gerbils, hamsters, rabbits, etc.). Each food is scientifically formulated to provide optimum nutrition and dietary balance for each kind of animal.

THE MARKET: Pet owners, animal breeders, and pet store owners (to feed the animals in their stores).

THE PACKAGE: Each food in the line is available in four packages: a 14 ounce box (4'' × 8'' × 2'') and five-, twenty-five-, and fifty-pound bags. All have identical coloration—salmon pink with dark-green type. The product name (i.e., GERBIL FOOD, FINCH FOOD, etc.) is spread across the middle of the package. A green palm leaf logo follows the ''PET PARADISE'' name on the bottom third.

DISTRIBUTION: Supermarkets (boxes), pet shops and discount chains (both boxes and bags).

PRICE: Same as its major competitor, the largest pet food distributor in the nation.

AD BUDGET: $500,000 annually.

MARKETING PROBLEM: Lack of consumer awareness has led to brand erosion.

1. Write a 60-second slice-of-life spot using sound effects.
2. Write a 30-second spinoff in any format.

RADIO SCRIPT SHEET

Student name: Advertiser:

Date submitted: Product:

Commercial length: Format:

Assignment 7-2: Background Data

THE CLIENT: Claussen's Catfish

THE PRODUCT: Claussen's catfish are carefully raised in fresh well-water ponds, or farms. They're fed a special formula of selected grains and grain products. This raising method produces a catfish that is lighter in color, flakier in texture, and more delicately flavored than ordinary catfish. (Some people compare it to Dover sole.) These fish are high in protein and low in cholesterol, calories, and fat. They are always sold fresh as uniform-sized whole fish, steaks, and fillets.

THE MARKET: The fish is purchased mostly by women, but it is eaten by people of both sexes and of all ages. The best geographical market is in the South and along the Mississippi River, where catfish are more commonly eaten. Claussen's Catfish is popular with dieters.

THE PACKAGE: All cuts are sold in random weights in light blue foam trays that are sealed in a clear poly wrap. Red diagonal printing—running from the upper right-hand corner to the lower left-hand corner—includes the words ''CLAUSSEN'S CATFISH,'' ''FRESH,'' and ''FARM-RAISED.'' Cooking suggestions are printed in black on the lower right portion of the wrapper. The company logo is two ''C's'' linked together.

DISTRIBUTION: Nationwide in supermarkets, seafood shops; food brokers; institutional and restaurant suppliers.

PRICE: $2.99 per pound, comparable to trout and other better quality fish.

AD BUDGET: $150,000 annually.

MARKETING PROBLEM: Lack of trial has caused sluggish sales.

1. Write a 60-second testimonial without sound effects or music.
2. Write a 30-second musical that includes a jingle.

RADIO SCRIPT SHEET

Student name: Advertiser:

Date submitted: Product:

Commercial length: Format:

Assignment 7-3: Background Data

THE CLIENT: A-One Brake Service

THE PRODUCT: This independent service station offers complete repair service on all foreign and domestic cars, including brakes, front end, tires, transmissions, and exhaust systems. Six experienced mechanics are trained to do everything, from tune-up and lubrication to body work and painting. Service is fast and dependable. Prices are fair, and owner Mack Johnson, who has been at 6th and Fremont streets for more than 20 years, is friendly and accessible.

THE MARKET: A-One's main customers are businessmen and other white-collar workers who drive to their downtown offices and park their cars within a ten-block radius of the A-One shop. Competition includes one franchised dealer whose station does not offer a full line of car services and a run-down independent station that offers inexpensive but dependable work, especially on American-made cars.

THE PACKAGE: A-One is an efficiently run operation. Mechanics wear uniforms, and the shop is kept as clean as possible.

DISTRIBUTION: The downtown area of Big Bluff, Illinois, population 140,000.

PRICE: All service and repair prices are competitive, but lower than those at the franchised shop and higher than those at the other privately owned station.

AD BUDGET: $5,000 annually.

MARKETING PROBLEM: Business at A-One Brake Service has declined because of a few well-publicized consumer complaints about the physical condition of the shop before its recent refurbishing.

1. Write a 60-second straight announcement in the spokesman format using music and/or sound effects.
2. Write a 30-second spinoff without embellishments.

RADIO SCRIPT SHEET

Student name: Advertiser:

Date submitted: Product:

Commercial length: Format:

Assignment 7-4: Background Data

THE CLIENT: Miller & Webb

THE PRODUCT: Miller & Webb men's clothing store has made a special purchase of 1,500 dress shirts. The manufacturer of the high-quality shirts, a nationally known advertiser, has given Miller & Webb a special price in order to reduce surplus stock. The shirts are current styles in a variety of solid colors and stripes. All have long sleeves and two-button cuffs. The fabric is "no iron" broadcloth of 65% polyester and 35% cotton.

THE MARKET: Men, 18 years old and over. Competitors can offer equal quality but not comparable prices.

THE PACKAGE: The shirts will bear the national advertiser's label. Miller & Webb is an upscale men's shop located in a suburban Atlanta shopping mall.

DISTRIBUTION: Miller & Webb's mall outlet.

PRICE: $20.00 each.

AD BUDGET: $3,000 in radio for this promotion.

MARKETING PROBLEM: Consumers are unaware of the store's offer of high-quality merchandise at low prices.

1. Write a 60-second spot in the spokesman format using one of the store owners.
2. Write a 30-second straight announcement delivered by a paid spokesperson.

RADIO SCRIPT SHEET

Student name: Advertiser:

Date submitted: Product:

Commercial length: Format:

Assignment 7-5: Marketing Objectives

MARKETING: For many years a life insurance company, Prudential has extended its coverage to property and casualty. The marketing goal is to create an awareness among adults that Prudential agents can provide automobile and homeowner as well as life insurance through Prudential's new property and casualty divisions.

ADVERTISING: Prudential wishes to announce its new businesses and familiarize the public with the name of its new divisions: Prudential Property and Casualty Insurance Co. The advertising should also state that the company may be able to save the consumer money on car and home insurance. Present life-insurance policy holders can deal with their current agent. And potential buyers can now take care of all their insurance needs at Prudential. The long-standing theme of the company's advertising has been: ''Get a piece of the rock.'' The corporate logo is a circle enclosing an illustration of the Rock of Gibraltar.

1. Write a 60-second commercial in the slice-of-life format.
2. Write a 30-second spinoff in any format.

RADIO SCRIPT SHEET

Student name: Advertiser:

Date submitted: Product:

Commercial length: Format:

Assignment 7-6: Marketing Objectives

MARKETING: A large and successful food manufacturing company has decided to market a new product called Sweet 'n Tart cranberry sauce. The marketing objective is to achieve year-round sales. Traditionally, cranberry sauce has been used by housewives only on holiday occasions, such as Thanksgiving and Christmas.

ADVERTISING: The campaign should make consumers think of serving cranberry sauce throughout the year. The association with Thanksgiving and turkey should be avoided. The product should be associated with other holidays or seasons and with a variety of foods, ranging from ham and cold cuts to steak and lamb chops.

1. Write a 60-second spot in any format using any combination of special elements.
2. Write a 30-second spinoff.

RADIO SCRIPT SHEET

Student name: Advertiser:

Date submitted: Product:

Commercial length: Format:

Assignment 7-7: Fact Sheet

Many advertisers take advantage of the skills of local deejays and/or announcers who are particularly adept at ad-libbing. Rather than restrict them to following a script, they are given fact sheets about the product or service. It is then up to each announcer to provide a lead-in, lace the different sales points together, provide persuasive word-pictures, and end with a strong bid for action. The fact sheet below, prepared for the Australian Trade Commission, supplies the names, description, and uses for the products to be advertised in an extemporaneous spot.

Products: Australian apples and pears

1. A fresh supply of Australian apples and pears has just arrived.
2. Two varieties of pears are Bosc and Parkhams (Park-ums).
3. Both are sweet and succulent and have a distinctive taste.
4. They may look like domestic pears, but their taste is superior—their flesh is white and aromatic.
5. Pears shipped to the U.S. are the best of a vintage crop.
6. The apples are called "Granny Smith" apples.
7. Green in color, they are nevertheless magnificent eating apples.
8. These apples can also be used in cooking.
9. Now available in grocery stores and supermarkets at a price about the same as domestic apples and pears.
10. More and more people are asking for them, so hurry—before they are sold out.

1. Write a 30-second commercial in the spokesman format.
2. Write a 30-second spot in another format.

RADIO SCRIPT SHEET

Student name: Advertiser:

Date submitted: Product:

Commercial length: Format:

Assignment 7-8: Rewrite

This radio commercial used an actual disaster as the basis for a compelling message: Despite a fire that destroyed the agency's offices and equipment, the company was still in business. While the spokesman format worked well, the "good news" could have been communicated in other ways. First read the script and then do the assignments below.

1. Write a 60-second revision of this commercial in a spokesman/interview format.
2. Write a 60-second problem-solution commercial using sound effects.

ANNCR: This is a message to the people who burned down our office building the day before Christmas. Contrary to reports in the media, Martin/Williams Advertising was not one of seven businesses destroyed by the fire you set. You burned our offices, you burned our furniture, you burned our equipment and you burned a lot of valuable personal things. But you didn't put us out of business. Two days after you set the fire we found temporary office space. . .slightly worn, but usable. Three days after you set the fire we salvaged all our financial records, all our media records, most of our art files. . .we moved them into our new space. Four days after the fire, including a day off for Christmas, we were hard at work producing advertising for our clients. We don't know why you set the fire. Whatever your motivation, we're pretty burned up about it. But we're not burned out. We're still open for business, still actively seeking new business. Martin/Williams Advertising. Temporarily located at 909 Hennepin Avenue in the Pence Building. Right next door to the fireproof hotel.

RADIO SCRIPT SHEET

Student name: Advertiser:

Date submitted: Product:

Commercial length: Format:

Assignment 7-9: Rewrite

The following carefully written and effectively delivered 30-second spot worked its magic without music, dramatic story, or sound effects. With a deep, resonant voice, the spokesman successfully communicated the "ferocity" of the product by emphasizing the words "kills" and "croak." Examine the script and then revise it according to the directions below.

1. Write a 30-second revision of this spot in a problem-solution format. Add special effects.
2. Write a 30-second version in any other format.

ANNCR: In the beginning there was soap and water... then came medicated cleansers. And now there's Oxy Wash with 10% benzoyl peroxide....It actually helps prevent pimples. While Oxy Wash gently washes away dirt and oil, its benzoyl peroxide kills acne bacteria with a ferocity unequaled in modern face washing. Want to help prevent tomorrow's pimples today? Then don't just soak your acne bacteria, croak them.... Wash with Oxy Wash.

RADIO SCRIPT SHEET

Student name: Advertiser:

Date submitted: Product:

Commercial length: Format:

Assignment 7-10: Rewrite

The TV script below was created to introduce a new, exclusive style of Mott's apple sauce, Golden Delicious Chunky. It was also used in certain markets as a wedge to gain distribution of other Mott's styles. The advertising was intended to show consumers that Mott's makes the style of apple sauce they like—and makes it better. Read the script carefully and then rewrite it as directed.

1. Rewrite this TV spot as a 30-second testimonial for radio.
2. Rewrite it as a 30-second musical.

BOY STANDING NEXT TO TABLE
WITH FOUR JARS OF MOTT'S ON
IT. BOY TAKES INTRODUCTORY
BOW.

BOY (FACING CAMERA):   Apple Sauce by Mott's ... the best apple sauce in the whole world is made by Mott's.

BOY (WITH ECU OF JAR
AND BOWL):   There's Mott's regular ...

SILENCE WITH ECU OF BOY
TASING

BOY (WITH ECU OF JAR
AND BOWL):   and Mott's Low Calorie ...

SILENCE WITH ECU OF BOY
TASTING

BOY (WITH ECU OF JAR
AND BOWL):   and Cinnamon ... Cinnamon Flavored Country Style ...

SILENCE WITH ECU OF BOY
TASTING

BOY (WITH ECU OF JAR
AND BOWL):   and a new one ... Golden Delicious.

WOMAN (V.O.):   Very good, Tommy....New Mott's Golden Delicious Chunky with little chunks of golden delicious apple.

BOY (TASTING, WITH NAME
SUPERED):   And you thought Mott's just made regular apple sauce....

RADIO SCRIPT SHEET

Student name: Advertiser:

Date submitted: Product:

Commercial length: Format:

Assignment 7-11: Rewrite

This half-page print ad is dominated by the headline. Illustration and copy are kept to a minimum. Staying with the primary selling theme, revise the ad for use on radio according to the directions given below.

1. Write a 30-second spot in the slice-of-life format.
2. Write a 30-second commercial in the problem-solution format.

TAKE THE SHOCK OUT OF YOUR ELECTRIC BILL.

Introducing the new Frigidaire Frost-Proof Refrigerators.

The most energy efficient refrigerators we've ever made.

In fact, our Frost-Proof line is the most energy efficient line of frost free refrigerators in the industry.

So efficient they start saving you money on your electric bill the minute you plug one in.

Savings that grow day after day. Month after month. Year after year.

FRIGIDAIRE
HERE TODAY, HERE TOMORROW

RADIO SCRIPT SHEET

Student name: Advertiser:

Date submitted: Product:

Commercial length: Format:

The full-page magazine ad below follows the company's slogan, "A breed apart," in both headline and illustration (a bull and a beacon). The long copy focuses on one Merrill Lynch product: certificates of deposit. Note that readers are urged to call for information or visit an account executive. Rewrite this ad for radio as directed.

1. Write a 60-second version of this ad in any format.
2. Write a 30-second spot in the spokesman format.

Who discovered
whole new ways to guide
investors to safety?

Who else but
Merrill Lynch.

Certificates of Deposit are as safe as money in the bank—they're insured for up to $100,000 by FDIC or FSLIC.

But Merrill Lynch has gone an important step beyond simply offering you the safety of CD's. Now our Account Executives can help you use them *strategically.* We have pioneered a new program of participations in federally insured 6 month, $100,000 CD's issued by national banks or S&L's.

Because rates on these jumbo CD's are not regulated, the participations pay higher interest than 6 month money market certificates are permitted to. And the minimum investment is only $1000.

Now, here's the strategic part. If you think interest rates are going up, you can take advantage of it with a participation in a 6-month *variable-rate* CD. But if you think rates are going to fall, you can lock in today's yields with a participation in a 6 month *fixed-rate* CD.

Whichever you choose, you get one added benefit: liquidity. Although not obliged to do so, Merrill Lynch intends to maintain a secondary market in all CD participations we sell.*

For a copy of our booklet, *Insured CD Participations,* call 1-800-MERRILL (ext. 952) Monday through Friday, 8:30 a.m. to midnight Eastern time.

Or talk to a Merrill Lynch Account Executive. No one else can give you more help with more kinds of investments. No one else.

Merrill Lynch

Merrill Lynch, Pierce, Fenner & Smith Inc.
A breed apart.

RADIO SCRIPT SHEET

Student name: Advertiser:

Date submitted: Product:

Commercial length: Format:

Section Three:
Television Commercials

Dimensions 8

When television began in the early 1940s, no one doubted that this new medium would have a significant impact on American society. After all, it combined the broadcasting power of radio and the well-established appeal of "talkie" movies. That is, it promised to bring already popular forms of entertainment—vaudeville, live theater, and films—into everyone's living room. And it would do all this for free.

Yet, if anything, the influence of television was vastly underestimated. It has affected the lives—and lifestyles—of the American people more than any other innovation in mass communications except the printing press. And it is probably at least equal in cultural impact to those other wonders of the 20th century—the automobile and the computer.

Thanks to television, millions of people have been entertained regularly by internationally famous stars, spectacular stage productions, and a constant flow of less grandiose, but otherwise unavailable, musical, dramatic, and comic performances. And TV has provided more than entertainment. Television has made instant and extensive news coverage and analysis part of the daily and nightly diet of millions of viewers through regularly scheduled morning and evening news programs. It brought the Vietnam War into the homes of Americans—daily, graphically, and powerfully. It made nearly every television owner an integral part of the first U.S. manned missle launch to the moon. And it transformed the political process by making it almost mandatory for candidates for national office to appear, speak, and debate before the penetrating eye of the TV camera.

With all this to offer, television profoundly changed the social habits of all Americans. Attendance at movie theaters plummeted drastically in the 1950s as a direct result of TV's growing popularity. Small-town inhabitants abandoned Main Street on weekend nights for television's then modest fare. And families everywhere, it is said, gave up conversation in exchange for a few hours of silence in front of the television screen.

Even TV commercials have become an important part of the American scene. Network news programs, local radio talk shows, front-page newspaper articles, and magazine feature stories are constantly telling people about television advertising—about unusual campaigns, new commercial celebrities, expensive talent contracts, and technological innovations. Even advertising agency negotiations for running TV campaigns for presidential candidates have attracted the interest of a public whose fascination with the medium seems insatiable—and growing.

Television Today

At the start of the 1950s, fewer than one in ten American households had a television set. Ten years later, set penetration approached the 90 percent level. Today, more than 98 percent of all U.S. homes have TV sets; about 77 percent have more than one receiver; and about 57 percent have more than two. Approximately 75,000,000 sets are color. According to A. C. Nielsen statistics, the average American watches slightly more than seven hours of TV a day. A study by the Roper Organization shows that 67 percent turn to television daily as their primary source of news and that nearly half rank TV as the most believable news source.

On the negative side, commercial television is not without its problems. Probably the most important challenge it faces is the decline in its share of viewership brought about by the growth and development of cable/pay TV and its limitless variations. This loss began in 1980 and promised to continue for at least the next decade. The cable networks have something unique to offer: specialized programing aired at specific, though smaller, audiences. Today, there are about 18 major advertiser-supported cable networks and more than 100 multiple system cable operators. These 100 operators control 5,400 individual cable systems across the country. Two-thirds of the nation, or 56,000,000 out of 83,000,000 homes, have been wired for cable. Almost one-third of U.S. homes currently subscribe to cable television systems.

Visionaries have predicted that a 108-channel system will eventually be available to every TV set. In fact, in 1984, Chicago was franchised to wire 104 channels. However, there seems to be only enough commercial-generating programing to fill a very small percentage of these channels. And many of them will therefore be limited to noncommercial programing. As of the mid-1980s, viewer response to pay-per-view TV has been disappointing. Evidently, cable subscribers do not want to pay an added premium to view one-time feature events (sports, movies, concerts). Videotex and Teletext, the much-heralded two-way cable systems, are costly, and consumers seem loath to pay for home banking and shopping, video games, and news.

In the future, other technologies that will compete with cable—such as microwave facilities, Satellite Master Antenna (SMATV), and Direct Broadcast Satellite (DBS)—will pose a threat to cable's market because they can be built faster and more cheaply. However, they have the disadvantages of fewer channels, weather interference, and higher subscriber costs.

Television Advertising

There are many who question the psychological and cultural benefits of television. However, few can deny that, for better or worse, television has transformed American life, especially the consumer marketplace. Television reaches big numbers of people with big impact at big costs. And it involves big risks and equally big rewards. The cost of producing a one-hour TV show, such as "Dallas," is about $600,000. One 30-second commercial during the 1984 Super Bowl reached 100,000,000 viewers at a cost of $450,000— and that's not counting the expense of producing a half-minute spot, which averages $100,000.

Of course, to be fair, you must compare the advertising costs of television to the costs of other media. For example, an ad in *Reader's Digest,* which reaches about 55,000,000 readers, costs more than $100,000. In fact, although the costs of creating, producing, and airing a TV commercial are staggering, television is one of the most cost-efficient media. And when you factor in the impact of a TV spot—as compared to that of a radio commercial or a magazine ad—it becomes clear that no other medium lets you reach and *influence* so many people at so little cost per person. For about four or five dollars, you can have a personal salesman call on a thousand potential customers, show them your product, demonstrate its effectiveness, and ask for an order. This advertising power has built brands that were unheard of before the advent of TV into national leaders, including Crest, Marlboro, Certs, and Clorets. Small wonder that considerable care and expertise should be given the preparation of every TV commercial.

Advertising on cable/pay TV will become increasingly important as new research techniques enable advertisers to find out the size of the audience and its demographic and psychographic composition. It appears that cable TV will become a "magazine stand" of the air. Because each cable/pay TV channel caters to a highly segmented audience with specific wants and needs, commercials have to be written to address these segments.

Advantages

Over the last three decades, television has shown itself to offer advertisers several distinct advantages over other media. Of course, its most outstanding attribute, which no other medium can match, is its ability to reach vast numbers of consumers in one shot. Other advantages are impact, credibility, selectivity, and flexibility.

1. *Television is powerful.* TV has the strengths of all the major media. Like direct mail, it comes directly *to* the consumer—in his home. Like radio, it offers sound, including special effects as well as music. And like print, it can show the product alone, in a setting, or in use. Furthermore, unlike any other advertising vehicle, television can portray the product in motion—whether it is poured, driven, eaten, worn, or otherwise consumed. This means that the viewer actually sees the product in "real life," which means that TV can present its sales message far more forcefully than any other medium.

2. *Television is believable.* Although some viewers regard TV advertising as exaggerated and misleading, the medium has an undeniable capacity to induce belief because, as the old saying goes, seeing is believing. Viewers can actually see product users succeed where they have formerly failed, smile with satisfaction, and receive the visible and tangible rewards of success— praise, gratitude, and approval.

Furthermore, products can be demonstrated. Viewers can be shown how they work, what they do, and why they should be purchased. Advertisers can demonstrate how products perform in comparison with other products. And they can show products undergoing tests that "prove" their claims for effectiveness, strength, or durability. Other media can only report the results, not display them and thereby subject them to public scrutiny and judgment.

3. *Television is selective.* TV can reach any target audience—any age group and any demographic segment. Commercials aimed at children can be spotted on after-school programs; those directed at housewives can be shown with daytime dramas; and adult male viewers can be reached at night through commercials on sports shows. Spot TV allows both the national chain store and the national advertiser to advertise in markets in which a store or product needs extra support or in which potential sales are greatest.

4. *Television is flexible.* Advertisers can purchase time on TV locally, regionally, or nationally. Thus, television can be used by both local and national companies. Small, independent retailers can use local TV production facilities at comparatively low cost. And national advertisers can broadcast their selling messages from coast to coast or in selected local markets.

Guidelines

You'll find a use for many of your skills when you create a TV commercial: the playwright's way with words, the artist's eye, the director's touch, the psychologist's understanding of human motivation, and the salesman's ability to convince. Any one of these might tend to overbalance the others, so add your sense of judgment to obtain the proper mix.

Your aim is to create a TV commercial with a powerful selling idea developed with imagination and presented with unity, coherence, and structure. To help you reach this goal, we have provided some general guidelines. They should serve to keep you aware of the medium's strengths and limitations and of the important target—the TV viewer you hope to reach, attract, and convince.

1. *Do your basic research first.* Get the facts—all the facts you can—about the product or service you are to advertise. And don't neglect either the competition or the consumer. Make sure you know what you're up against and whom you're trying to reach.

2. *Emphasize your main selling point.* Analyze your research and then crystallize it into major and minor selling points. Focus on the strongest, most provocative possibility for a selling idea—and stress that one.

3. *Make your commercial relevant.* It must relate to viewer wants and needs. Make it meaningful to him in his own terms. Along with your native imagination and creativity, use taste and discretion. Respect your viewer's sensitivity and intelligence.

4. *Get attention fast—and keep it.* The opening seconds of a spot are vital. These either grab and hold viewer attention or turn it off. But don't just surprise or shock. As soon as possible, let the viewer know what's in it for him. Remember, although your ad gains by going after attention, it must hold on to it in order to convince and sell.

5. *Match medium and message.* The format, structure, and style of your commercial should be compatible with each other and with the product. Also, be sure to match video and audio. They must relate to each other throughout the spot, or you'll confuse the viewer.

6. *Stay on track.* While you are developing the elements of your commercial, check back frequently with your strategy statement and marketing objectives.

7. *Don't waste words.* Television is primarily a visual medium, so your video directions should carry more than half the weight of your message. Which come first, words or pictures? That depends on your own creativity. Try it both ways. Try to visualize as you write, and vice versa. Video instructions should be specific and exact. You'll only get what you ask for.

8. *Keep your commercial simple.* Do not cram your spot with too many scenes or too much movement. How much is too much? That depends on the type of spot you are creating. A spot using the spokesman

format needs few scenes. A narrative may require many. On the other hand, avoid long, static scenes. Provide for *some* movement of camera and/or actors.

9. *Be prepared to revise.* Don't expect to write a final script on the first try. True professionals rewrite and polish material again and again. At some point during the job of writing or sketching your storyboard, you may think of other ways to do the commercial. One of them may be an improvement. If it is, start all over again with it.

Once you are satisfied with your script or storyboard, set it aside. Become a devil's advocate. Look at the script later as objectively as you can. Examine it for impact, clarity, rhythm, pace, persuasion, relevance, and believability. If you do not score well on all of these points, revise.

10. *Write clearly and conversationally.* Write your copy in a natural manner. Avoid the pretentious and the glib. Remember, you are trying to talk to one person whom you don't really know. To paraphrase Shakespeare, "Suit the word to the action"—the mood of the commercial and the personality of the product.

11. *Identify your product.* One of the main reasons why the majority of TV commercials are ineffective is that the brand name has not been implanted strongly. People often recall a bit of action and sometimes remember the product category. But unless you have made a special point of saying—and repeating—the name, it won't stay in your viewer's mind and therefore won't motivate him to buy the product.

12. *Time your commercial.* Read it aloud. Act it out. Don't rush it. A pace too fast for the announcer or actor will deprive your spot of its dramatic appeal. And a pace too fast for the viewer will leave him far behind.

TV commercials come in varying lengths: 10, 15, 20, 30, and 45 seconds and one or two minutes. On the average, shorter commercials register as well and sometimes better than longer ones. From a creative point of view, the length of the spot is relatively unimportant. Certainly, you can get more frills into a 60-second commercial than you can in a 10-second one. But it has been proven over and over again that you can deliver a powerful message in a short commercial as effectively as you can in a long one. Of course, the key ingredient, the selling idea, must be presented in a memorable, emphatic way, no matter how long or short the commercial is.

13. *Treat news as news.* If your product is new or has a new feature, give your commercial an announcement flavor. Like newspaper readers, TV viewers appreciate and show interest in something new.

14. *Repeat yourself.* Purposeful repetition can help register a selling idea. Don't expect the viewer to remember it if you say or show it only once in a 60-second spot.

15. *Concentrate on writing, not drawing.* A beautifully drawn storyboard is no substitute for a good

selling idea. Storyboards are adequate if they are drawn with stick figures—as long as the idea, along with structure and continuity, comes through.

16. *Give some free rein to the producer.* The storyboard is merely a blueprint. It is prepared so that you and others can better visualize the commercial. The producer should not be completely locked in to every shot shown in the storyboard. Everyone, from the writer to the producer, should have the constant assignment of trying to make the commercial better, even after final approval.

The TV Storyboard

A building contractor relies on an architect's specifications and blueprints. A commercial producer relies on a script and a storyboard. Radio commercials require scripts that provide copy and describe sound effects, music, and stage directions. Because it is visual as well as auditory, television needs not only a script, but also an artist's rendering of each scene. This rendering is called a storyboard.

As you will note in your study of TV commercial examples in Chapter 9, each frame in the storyboard presents a continuation of some action, a completely new scene, or an addition, such as a superimposed title. However, the storyboards in Chapter 9 are taken from the finished films, whereas actual storyboards (as opposed to photoboards) are rendered in varying degrees of "finish" (see Exhibits 8-1, 8-2, and 8-3). They are drawn in pencil, felt pen, drawing pen, or wash. Sometimes, photographs are used. When they are completed, storyboards show supervisors, clients, and commercial producers everything they need to know about what will be heard and seen, including locations, sets, actors, special effects, and titles.

A TV storyboard may consist of only one frame to show what will happen in a 10-second spot. Or it may consist of dozens of frames to show what will happen in a commercial lasting a minute or longer. Video and audio instructions are placed under each frame.

The importance of a clear and understandable storyboard cannot be overemphasized. An easy-to-follow board will aid the evaluators in their approval or disapproval. A good idea with a good structure will show through even a poorly drawn board; conversely, a well-drawn board might also reveal the weakness of a bad idea or a confusing structure.

Storyboard Development

Storyboards can be developed by one person or by a team of two or more. Some creators of commercials combine the talents of both writer and artist. Some advertising agencies have teams of writer, artist, and producer join talents and create a commercial together. In this team effort, the writer can suggest visual treatments, and the artist can suggest copy changes. At its best, such teamwork stimulates free-wheeling creativity.

For the purpose of this book, assume that you are both writer and artist. It is not important that you be artistically skillful. If you lack drawing talent, use stick figures. With even rudimentary skills, you can indicate the scene, the number and types of people involved in each scene, and the proposed camera angles and distances, from close-up to long shot. However roughly you draw the frames, your storyboard will permit you—and others—to "see" the sequential flow of your commercial, to judge its structure, cohesiveness, and continuity.

In most agencies, a rough (basic) storyboard developed by a writer/artist will be reviewed by a producer (who advises on sets, techniques of camera work, and in-lab optical effects, etc.), creative supervisors, and account executives. It will then be sent, with corrections and changes, to the agency "bullpen." Here, the board will be drawn skillfully by sketchmen in a more comprehensive and finished form.

Many people are involved in either creating or passing judgment on the storyboard. If they are imaginative, their suggestions, embellishments, and improvements will show up in the finished product. When agency approval is won, the client's approval is sought. If granted, the commercial heads for production. The producer, director, and cameraman use the storyboard as a guide, a blueprint, and bring their combined expertise to bear.

Exhibit 8-1. Storyboard: American Federal

Advertiser: American Federal Savings

Agency: Fletcher/Mayo/Associates Inc.

Product: American Federal banking services

Title: ''Eagle''

Format: Analogy

Length: 30 seconds

Freedom.

It's the American Way. And that's the way at American Federal.

The freedom of express banking with one of our nearly 300 automatic teller machines.

Free 5 1/4% interest-paying checking with convenient pay-by-phone.

And a wide range of investment services

Stop by your nearby American Federal office.

Find out why you're better off having your banking and financial needs served the American way.

Exhibit 8-2. Storyboard: American Dairy Assn.

Advertiser: American Dairy Assn.

Agency: D'Arcy-MacManus & Masius

Product: Milk

Title: ''Dog Wash''

Formats: Slice of life/Musical

Length: 30 seconds

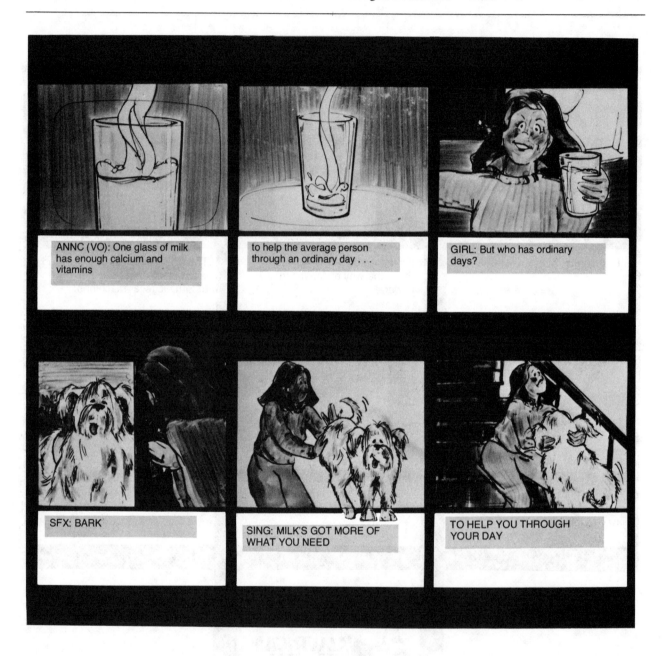

ANNC (VO): One glass of milk has enough calcium and vitamins

to help the average person through an ordinary day . . .

GIRL: But who has ordinary days?

SFX: BARK

SING: MILK'S GOT MORE OF WHAT YOU NEED

TO HELP YOU THROUGH YOUR DAY

MILK HELPS KEEP YOU GOING

WHEN THINGS DON'T GO YOUR WAY

ANNC (VO): Have an extra glass of milk. It gives you more of what you need

to help keep you going . . .

even through the messiest days!

SING: HAVE MORE MILK 'CAUSE MILK'S GOT MORE

Exhibit 8-3. Storyboard: Ar-Pac

Advertiser: Continental Animal Health

Agency: Ayres & Associates Inc.

Product: Ar-Pac disease preventive

Title: "Little Piggies"

Format: Spokesman

Length: 30 seconds

FARMER: You have to protect your pigs

(SFX: GATE OPENING) and your profits.

So I use AR-PAC and AR-PAC-P to fight rhinitis and pasteurella.

My dealer told me AR-PAC and AR-PAC-P are now improved with Gentamicin,

and that they come from the makers of Armidexan and Gleptosil.

Then he told me AR-PAC and AR-PAC-P were the first

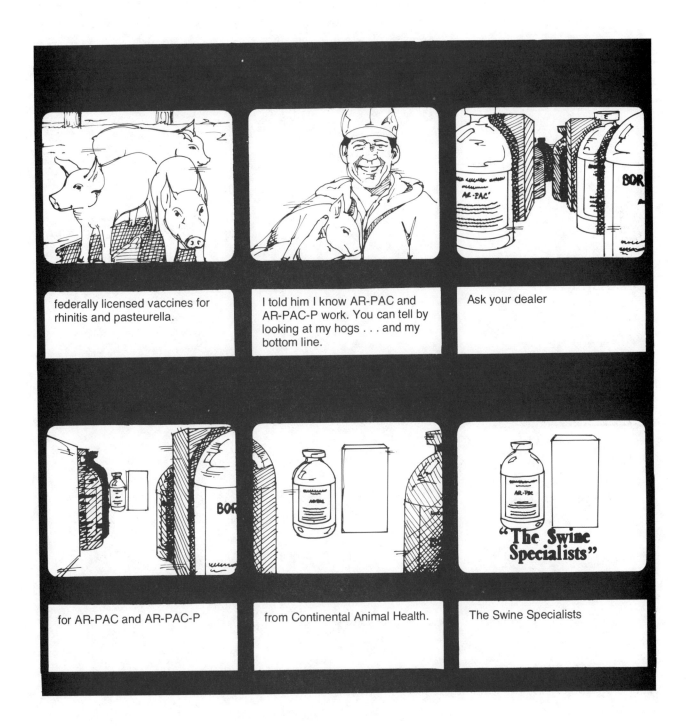

Examples 9

Like the radio spots in Chapter 6, the TV commercials in this chapter have been chosen for their excellence— their success in building product awareness, increasing dollar or unit sales, maintaining corporate image, and/ or establishing a desirable market position. All were broadcast either nationally or regionally.

Each format discussed in Chapter 3 is represented by one example. In addition, we have included several other commercials illustrating the use of particular structures (vignettes, continuing series), styles (fantasy, surrealism), and techniques (animation, computer graphics).

The special appeal of these commercials rests on their combination of strong selling idea, compatible format, and effective supplementary material. Analyze the strengths (and weaknesses, if any) of each spot, and try to determine the reasons for its success. Think of alternative ways of presenting the sales message. Would a different format work as well? Is the style appropriate? What techniques would you have used? What elements would you add to or delete from the commercial?

For each example, we have given the names of the advertiser, the agency, and the product; the title of the spot; the type of format; and the length.

Exhibit 9-1. Problem-Solution: IBM Datamaster

Advertiser: IBM

Agency: Doyle Dane Bernbach, Inc.

Product: Datamaster computer

Title: "Partners"

Format: Problem-solution

Length: 30 seconds

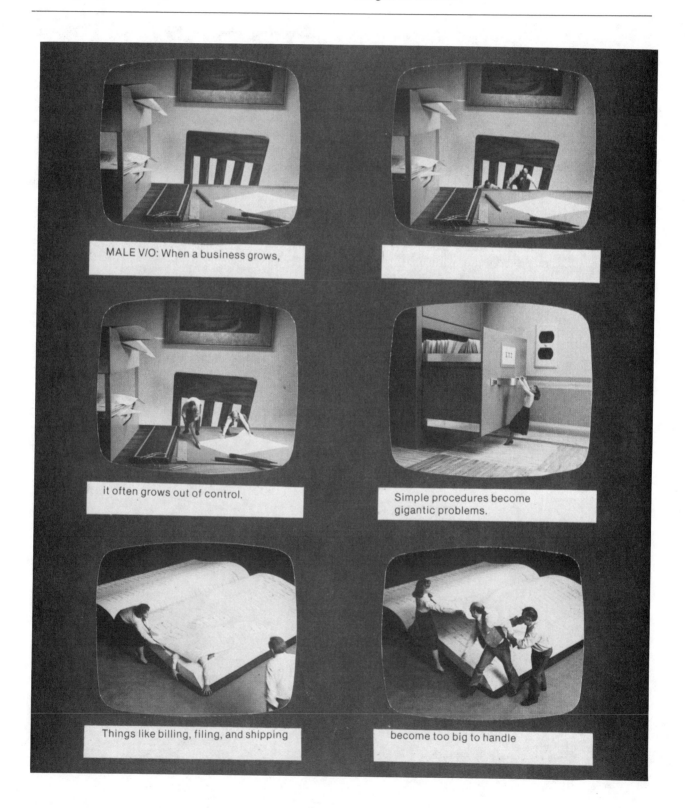

MALE V/O: When a business grows,

it often grows out of control.

Simple procedures become gigantic problems.

Things like billing, filing, and shipping

become too big to handle

the old way.

Why not get one of IBM's low-cost small computers -- like Datamaster?

It puts you back in control.

And it can grow --

MAN #2: Here's to a great future.
MALE V/O: . . . as your business grows.

Exhibit 9-2. Slice of Life: Crush

Advertiser: Crush International, Inc.

Agency: Cunningham & Walsh, Inc.

Product: Orange Crush soft drink

Title: "Orange Lovers"

Format: Slice of life

Length: 60 seconds

Music under BOY: C'mon Joey! JOEY: OK, I'll be right there. Hey listen, hold my Crush, but don't drink it. OK? LITTLE BROTHER: OK.

JOEY: Don't drink it! LITTLE BROTHER: I won't!

ANNCR (VO): Orange lovers have a crush on us

and you know why?

'Cause we've got 100% natural flavors.

JOEY: Don't drink it. LITTLE BROTHER: I won't.

ANNCR (VO): We're so orangey—

it makes us hard to resist.

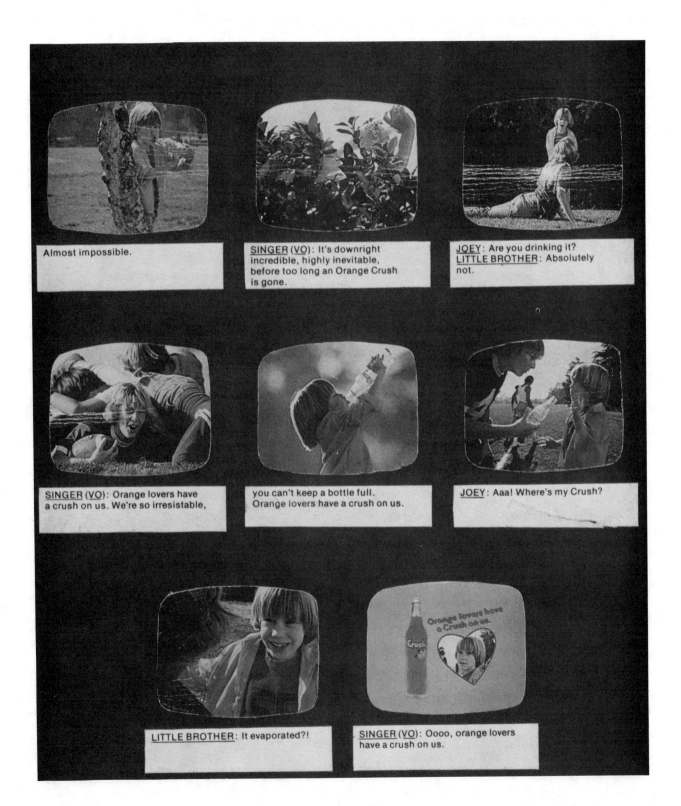

Almost impossible.

SINGER (VO): It's downright incredible, highly inevitable, before too long an Orange Crush is gone.

JOEY: Are you drinking it?
LITTLE BROTHER: Absolutely not.

SINGER (VO): Orange lovers have a crush on us. We're so irresistable,

you can't keep a bottle full. Orange lovers have a crush on us.

JOEY: Aaa! Where's my Crush?

LITTLE BROTHER: It evaporated?!

SINGER (VO): Oooo, orange lovers have a crush on us.

Exhibit 9-3. Narrative: Hallmark

Advertiser: Hallmark Cards, Inc.

Agency: Young & Rubicam

Product: Hallmark cards

Title: "Cards/Music Professor Surprise"

Format: Narrative

Length: 90 seconds

the right

surprise for you.

PROFESSOR: Good afternoon, Lisa.
LISA: Good afternoon, Professor.

PROFESSOR: Are we prepared?
LISA: I think so.

PROFESSOR: Hm, let's see

what Mr. Beethoven thinks.

(MUSIC)

LISA SINGS: (VO) So I'm giving you

this Hallmark and I hope that

you will see what I'm really giving you

is a part of me.

PROFESSOR: Thank you, Lisa.

ANNCR: (VO) Make someones's birthday special. Give a little of yourself.

Give a Hallmark card.

(MUSIC)

(MUSIC)

Exhibit 9-4. Demonstration: Canon "Snappy"

Advertiser: Canon U.S.A., Inc.

Agency: Grey Advertising, Inc.

Product: Canon "Snappy" camera

Title: "You Won't Believe Your Eyes"

Format: Demonstration

Length: 30 seconds

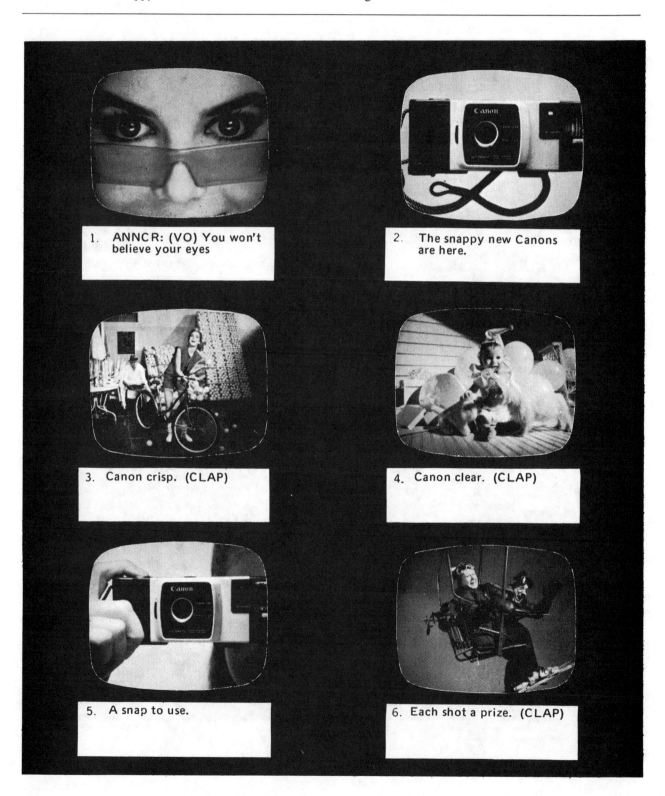

1. ANNCR: (VO) You won't believe your eyes

2. The snappy new Canons are here.

3. Canon crisp. (CLAP)

4. Canon clear. (CLAP)

5. A snap to use.

6. Each shot a prize. (CLAP)

7. You won't believe your eyes.

8. Canon quality photography

9. And the price? (CLAP)
   A nice surprise.

10. The snappy new Canons
    are here.

11. Thirty five millimeter.
    (CLAP) (CLAP) (CLAP)
    Crisp and clear.
    (CLAP) (CLAP) (CLAP)

12. You're in for a snappy
    surprise. You won't
    believe your eyes.

Exhibit 9-5. Product Alone: Burger King®

Advertiser: Burger King®

Agency: J. Walter Thompson USA

Product: Whopper sandwich

Title: ''H/Whopper We Know''

Format: Product alone

Length: 30 seconds

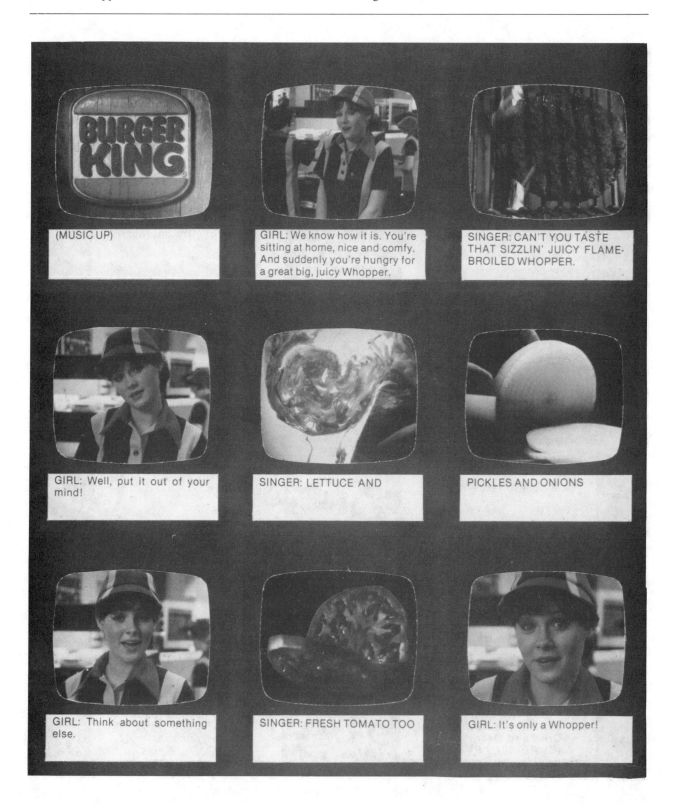

(MUSIC UP)

GIRL: We know how it is. You're sitting at home, nice and comfy. And suddenly you're hungry for a great big, juicy Whopper.

SINGER: CAN'T YOU TASTE THAT SIZZLIN' JUICY FLAME-BROILED WHOPPER.

GIRL: Well, put it out of your mind!

SINGER: LETTUCE AND

PICKLES AND ONIONS

GIRL: Think about something else.

SINGER: FRESH TOMATO TOO

GIRL: It's only a Whopper!

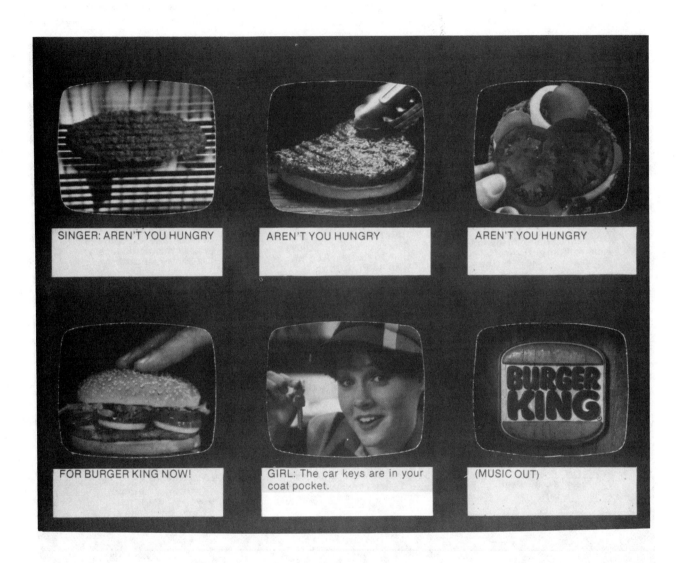

Exhibit 9-6. Spokesman: Chrysler

Advertiser: Chrysler Corp.

Agency: Kenyon & Eckhardt Inc.

Product: Chrysler corporate

Title: ''American Industry Rev.''

Format: Spokesman

Length: 60 seconds

1. LEE A. IACOCCA: There was a time when ''Made in America'' meant something. It meant you made the best.

2. Unfortunately a lot of Americans don't believe that anymore. And maybe with good reason,

3. but the time has come to restore the confidence of the American car buyer

4. in American technology, American workers and American cars.

5. It's time we in the auto industry convinced you that you can make a long-term investment

6. in the quality of a new American car and not have to worry about it.

7. So, Chrysler will protect every new American built Dodge, Chrysler and Plymouth passenger car 3 ways:

8. One: 5 years or 50,000 miles on engine and power train.

9. Two: 5 years or 50,000 miles rust proof protection on the outside of the car.

10. Three: 5 years or 50,000 miles free scheduled maintenance.

11. We in the car industry must make "Made in America" mean something again... we owe it to you.

12. So we invite GM and Ford to follow Chrysler. But until they do...

13. If you can find better protection, take it.

14. If you can find a better car, buy it.

15. (SILENT)

Exhibit 9-7. Testimonial: Miller Lite

Advertiser: Miller Brewing Co.

Agency: Backer & Spielvogel, Inc.

Product: Miller Lite beer

Title: ''Carlos Palomino''

Format: Testimonial

Length: 30 seconds

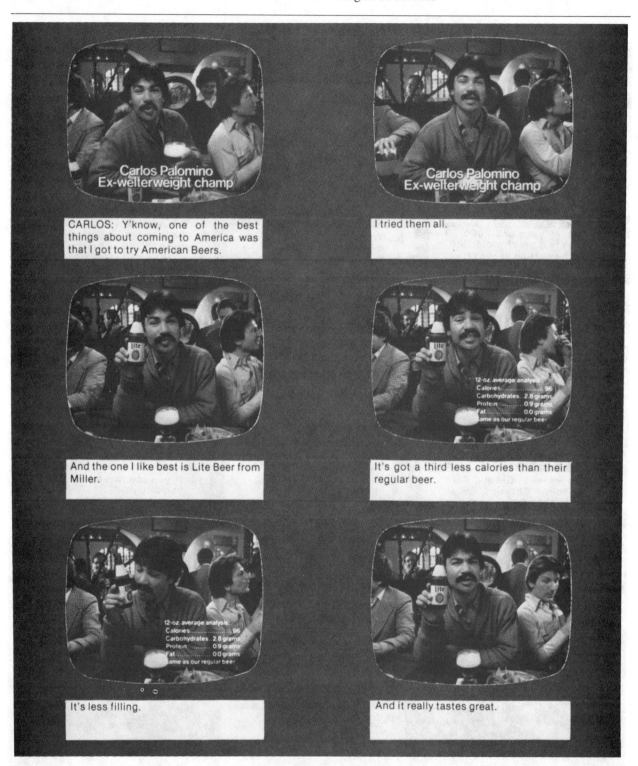

That is why I tell my friends from Mexico,

"When you come to America, drink Lite Beer.

But,

don't drink the water."

ANNCR: (VO) Lite Beer from Miller. Everything you always wanted in a beer.

And less.

Exhibit 9-8. Musical: 7UP

Advertiser: The Seven-Up Co.

Agency: J. Walter Thompson USA

Product: 7UP soft drink

Title: "Rear Window"

Format: Musical

Length: 30 seconds

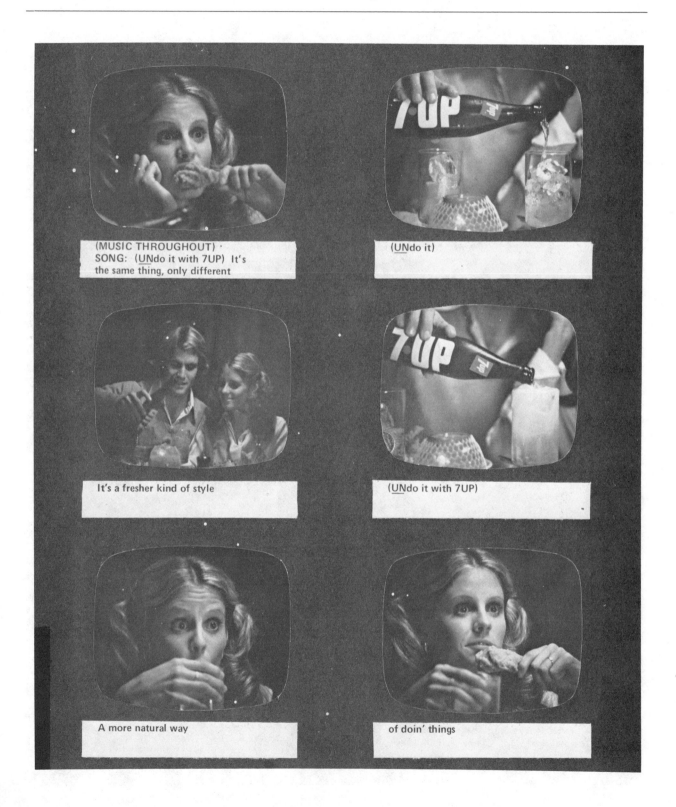

(MUSIC THROUGHOUT)
SONG: (UNdo it with 7UP) It's the same thing, only different

(UNdo it)

It's a fresher kind of style

(UNdo it with 7UP)

A more natural way

of doin' things

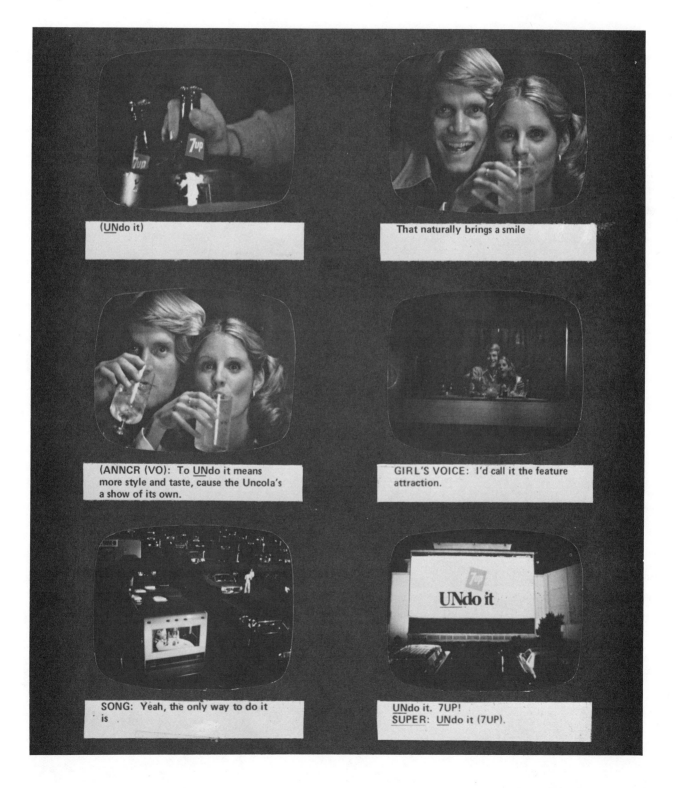

(UNdo it)

That naturally brings a smile

(ANNCR (VO): To UNdo it means more style and taste, cause the Uncola's a show of its own.

GIRL'S VOICE: I'd call it the feature attraction.

SONG: Yeah, the only way to do it is

UNdo it. 7UP!
SUPER: UNdo it (7UP).

Exhibit 9-9. Slice of Life/Continuing Series: Maytag

Advertiser: The Maytag Co.

Title: ''Pet''

Agency: Leo Burnett Co.

Formats: Slice of life/Continuing series

Product: Maytag washers

Length: 30 seconds

1. JESS: Pretty boy! Pretty boy!

2. PARROT: Pretty boy! (Screech) Pretty boy!

3. JESS: Every Maytag Repairman should have a nice pet like you. PARROT: (Squawk)

4. JESS: (Big sigh) Kinda takes my mind off of being lonely.

5. PARROT: Lonely! Lonely!

6. JESS: (Wistful) You see, it's these Maytag Washers...

7. ...they're really built. (Sfx: solid thunk)

8. JESS: (Helplessly) They're so darn dependable.

9. PARROT: Dependable! Dependable!

10. JESS: (Wistfully) You can
say that again.

11. PARROT: Dependable!
Dependable!

12. JESS: (Mildly) Alright do
you have to rub it in? ? ? ?

13. (Anncr VO) Not all Maytag
Repairmen are this lonely. But
we're trying.

14. Maytag,...

15. ...the dependability people.

Exhibit 9-10. Product Alone/Comparison: Heinz

Advertiser: H. J. Heinz Co.

Agency: Doyle Dane Bernbach, Inc.

Product: Heinz ketchup

Title: "Ketchup Race"

Formats: Product alone/Comparison

Length: 30 seconds

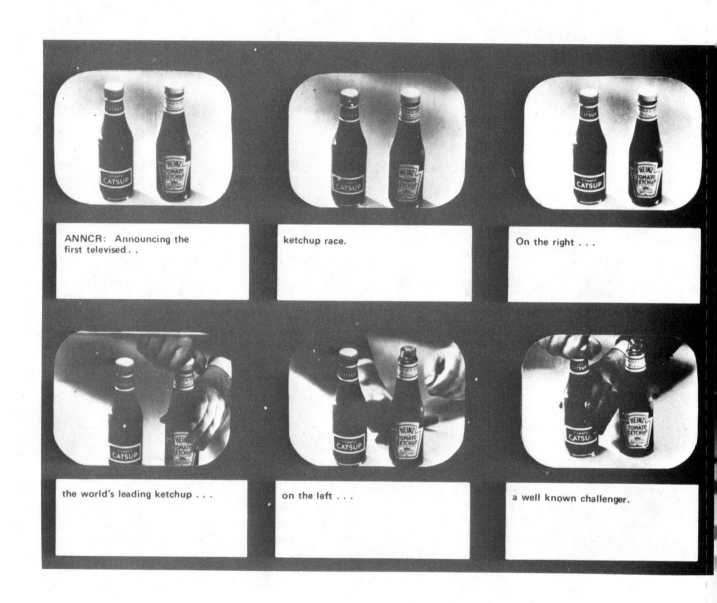

On your mark . . .

Get set . . .

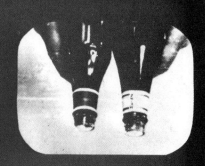

(SFX)

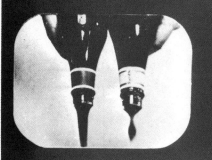

(SFX)

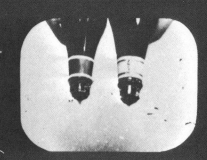

(SFX)

Heinz loses.

Heinz is too thick . . .

too rich . . .

to win a ketchup race.

Exhibit 9-11. Narrative/Fantasy: Chanel

Advertiser: Chanel, Inc.

Agency: Done in-house

Product: Chanel No. 5 perfume

Title: "Gardens"

Formats: Narrative/Fantasy

Length: 30 seconds

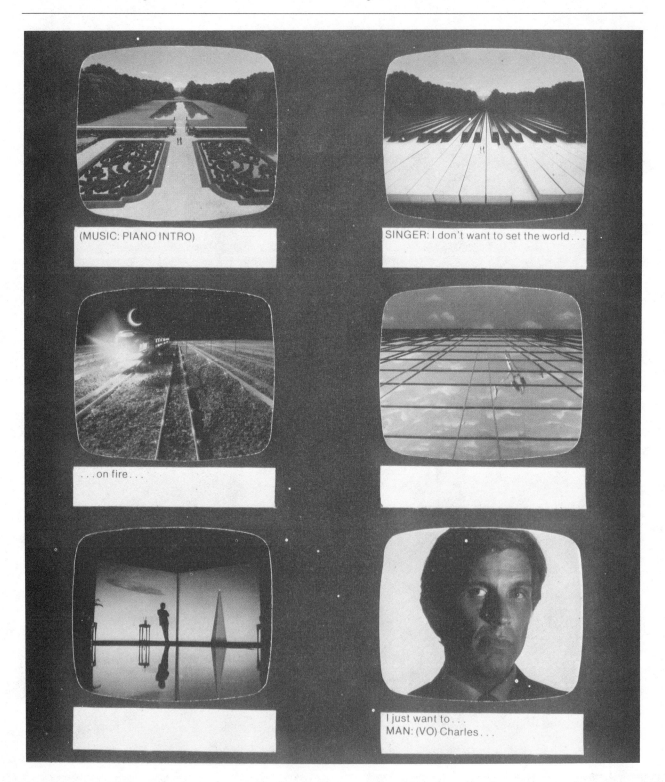

(MUSIC: PIANO INTRO)

SINGER: I don't want to set the world...

...on fire...

I just want to...
MAN: (VO) Charles...

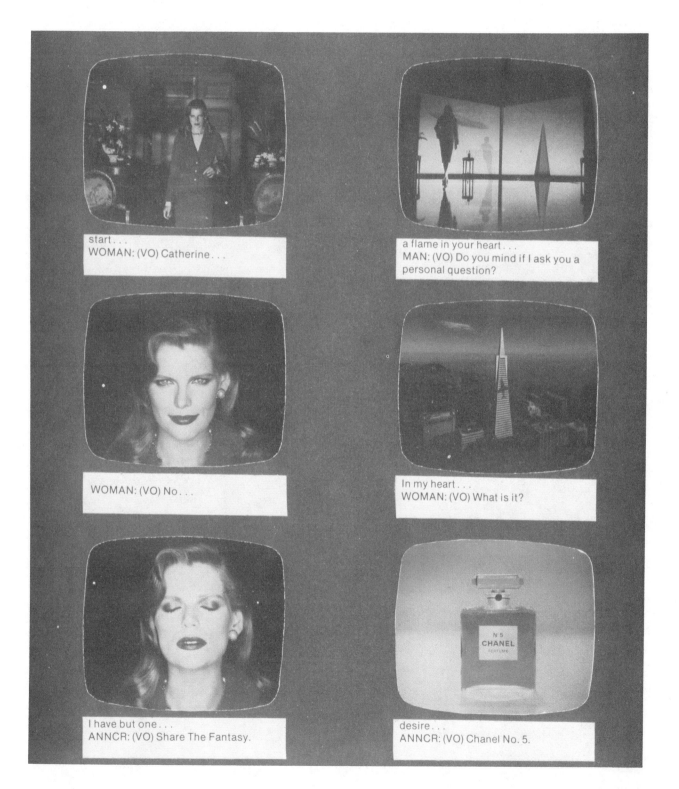

start . . .
WOMAN: (VO) Catherine . . .

a flame in your heart . . .
MAN: (VO) Do you mind if I ask you a
personal question?

WOMAN: (VO) No . . .

In my heart . . .
WOMAN: (VO) What is it?

I have but one . . .
ANNCR: (VO) Share The Fantasy.

desire . . .
ANNCR: (VO) Chanel No. 5.

Exhibit 9-12. Testimonial/Vignettes: Emery

Advertiser: Emery Worldwide	Title: ''Composite/FP''
Agency: Benton & Bowles	Formats: Testimonial/Vignettes
Product: Air freight delivery	Length: 30 seconds

(MUSIC UNDER)
JAPANESE MAN: Oh boka wa Emerii nijuu nenkan mo shinyoo shite orimasu.

FRENCH WOMAN: Merci.

C'est a Emery que je fais confiance depuis quinze ans.

GERMAN MAN: Danke Schoen.

Ich vertraue Emery weil sie immer schnell und zuverlassig sind.

AUSTRALIAN MAN: Emery First Class International door-to-door service. It's fast, mate.

ANNCR: (VO) Emery's been delivering around the world longer than most delivery companies have been around.

Call Emery. We've earned the trust of business worldwide.

Exhibit 9-13. Demonstration/Computer Graphics: SmithKline

Advertiser: SmithKline Corp.

Agency: Fletcher/Mayo/Assoc. Inc.

Product: Stafac growth promotant

Title: ''Slows the Feed . . .''

Format: Demonstration/Computer graphics

Length: 30 seconds

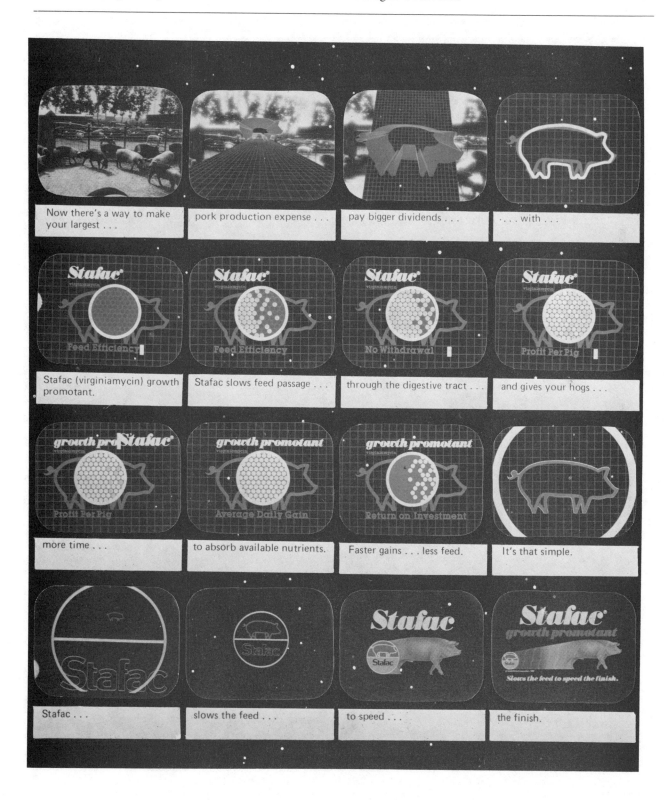

Now there's a way to make your largest . . .

pork production expense . . .

pay bigger dividends . . .

. . . . with . . .

Stafac (virginiamycin) growth promotant.

Stafac slows feed passage . . .

through the digestive tract . . .

and gives your hogs . . .

more time . . .

to absorb available nutrients.

Faster gains . . . less feed.

It's that simple.

Stafac . . .

slows the feed . . .

to speed . . .

the finish.

Exhibit 9-14. Slice of Life/Animation: Star-Kist

Advertiser: Star-Kist Foods, Inc.

Agency: Leo Burnett Co.

Product: Star-Kist tuna

Title: ''Ten More''

Format: Slice of life/Animation

Length: 30 seconds

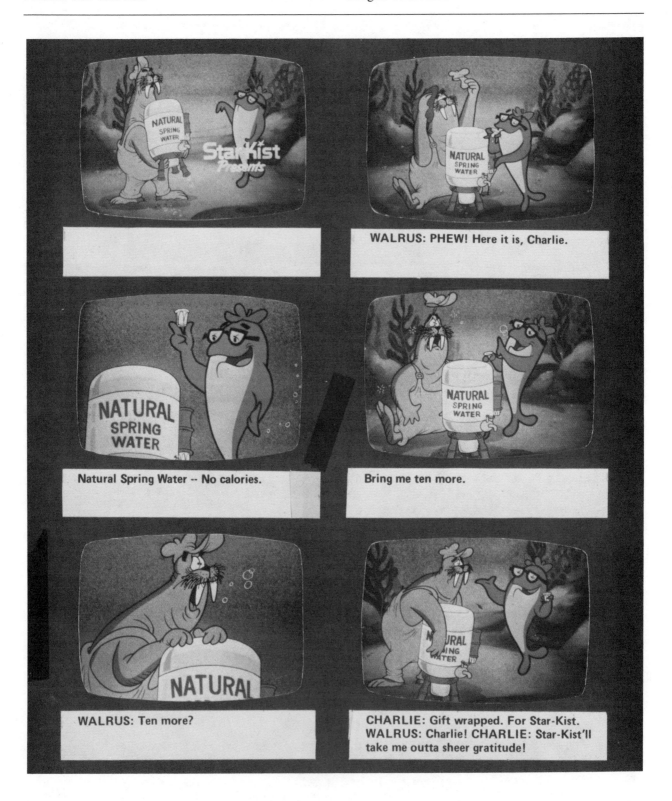

WALRUS: PHEW! Here it is, Charlie.

Natural Spring Water -- No calories.

Bring me ten more.

WALRUS: Ten more?

CHARLIE: Gift wrapped. For Star-Kist.
WALRUS: Charlie! CHARLIE: Star-Kist'll
take me outta sheer gratitude!

ANNCR: (VO) Star-Kist in Natural Spring Water.

Delicious taste, but half the calories of tuna in oil.

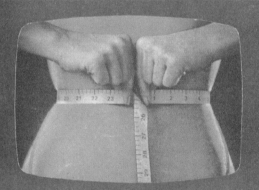

A measurable difference.

CHARLIE: Come and get your gifts, Star-Kist! ANNCR: (VO) Sorry Charlie.

Star-Kist Tuna in Natural Spring Water.

Good taste...naturally.

Assignments 10

Like those in Chapter 7, the assignments in this chapter will give you a chance to try your own hand at writing commercials. Of course, you should reexamine Chapters 2, 3, and 4 to reacquaint yourself with the fundamentals of writing and with the advertising elements you will be called upon to use. Remember, in writing television commercials, you have more techniques to work with and more elements to handle. For this reason, you must choose your components very carefully, with special attention to unity and coherence. It's very tempting to try to include too much. And it's not easy to get everything working together smoothly and effectively.

If you have trouble coming up with good ideas, review the guidelines in Chapter 8, and look over the TV commercials in Chapter 9. Don't be afraid to use a variation on someone else's idea—as long as it works.

Again, you will be asked to start with background data, a set of marketing/advertising objectives, or a print, TV, or radio ad. Spend a substantial amount of your creative time examining this material. Use it as a foundation for writing your strategy statement. And periodically check your developing commercial against the product facts, your objectives, and the selling theme contained in your strategy.

For each assignment, use the script sheet or storyboard form provided and follow the style shown in Chapter 9. Indicate advertiser, format, product and length. Double-space all assignments. Type names of speakers, sound effects, video directions, and music cues and copy in caps. Type nonmusical copy in upper and lower case letters. For TV scripts, follow the style shown in Exhibit 10-1. To get an idea of the kinds of questions you will have to answer, often *before* you have written a word of copy, examine Exhibit 10-2, which gives the production notes for the TV script in Exhibit 10-1.

Exhibit 10-1. TV Script: Coors Light

Advertiser: Adolph Coors Co. Title: "Camping"

Agency: Foote, Cone & Belding Format: Musical

Product: Coors Light beer Length: 60 seconds

VIDEO	AUDIO
OPEN ON BACK OF CAB, WEIGHED DOWN ON ONE SIDE.	(MUSIC UNDER)
CUT TO JIM, THE CAB DRIVER, IN A SERIES OF THREE PASSENGER SHOTS: HEAVY-SET WOMAN: BUSINESSMEN PILED INTO BACK SEAT, HOLDING A MEETING: A CAMERA-HAPPY TOURIST COUPLE.	JIM (VO): After the loads I carry all day, it's time to pick up speed.
CUT TO CAB DRIVING OUT OF FRAME.	
CUT TO "TURN IT LOOSE" NEON GRAPHIC.	SINGERS: TURN IT LOOSE,
VAN DRIVES INTO FRAME AND STOPS.	TURN IT LOOSE,
CUT TO JIM WITH COOLER. HE HITS VAN DOORS, HINGED SPEAKERS FALL DOWN.	TURN IT LOOSE TONIGHT.
CUT TO JIM TOSSING BEER TO HIS GIRL, SHERRY.	COORS LIGHT, COORS LIGHT
CUT TO UNENDING TRAIN OF FRIENDS CLIMBING OUT OF VAN, INCLUDING MOOSE, THE CHIPS-AND-BEER BUDDY.	TURN IT LOOSE TONIGHT.
CUT TO JIM LIGHTING FIRE, AS SHERRY WATCHES. HIS LIGHTER WON'T WORK, SO HE USES A BLOW TORCH.	DON'T HOLD BACK,
CUT TO TENT ALMOST UP.	DON'T HOLD BACK,
CUT TO JIM TURNING UP STEREO VOLUME.	TURN IT
CUT TO FRIEND, SAM, CONTENT TO SPEND THE EVENING IN THE VAN, TURNING UP VOLUME.	LOOSE TONIGHT.
CUT TO ELDERLY COUPLE, SURPRISED AT THE NOISE.	(COORS LIGHT)
CUT TO SHOT OF SHERRY SITTING ON COOLER. PEOPLE TAKE BEERS FROM COOLER, AS SHE SCOOTS UP AND DOWN (ALA CHOW-CHOW-CHOW).	BEER AFTER BEER WHEN YOU'RE MOVING AROUND
CU COORS LIGHT CAN WITH SWEAT DRIPPING	COORS LIGHT
CUT TO JIM AND FRIENDS, WITH SURPRISED LOOKS.	IS THE ONE
CUT TO THE TENT, COLLAPSING, WITH A FIGURE OF SOMEONE UNDERNEATH. A FLASHLIGHT TURNS ON.	THAT WON'T SLOW YOU DOWN.

CUT TO CU COORS LIGHT CAN BEING HELD.	COORS LIGHT
CUT TO MOOSE EMERGING FROM TENT, WITH CHIPS AND BEER INTACT.	TURN IT LOOSE TONIGHT.
CUT TO JIM, SEATED ON TINY CAMPING STOOL. HE LAUGHS SO HARD, HE FALLS OVER BACKWARD.	TURN IT LOOSE
CUT TO ELDERLY COUPLE, WITH BEERS, LAUGHING.	(LAUGHTER)
CUT TO CU COORS LIGHT CAN BEING OPENED. SUPER: TURN IT LOOSE!	SINGERS: TURN IT LOOSE!
	(COORS LIGHT!)

Exhibit 10-2. TV Production Notes: Coors Light

<u>PRODUCTION NOTES</u>

<u>OBJECTIVE</u>:

To produce a 30-second television commercial as part of Pool II for the existing Coors Light "Turn it loose!" campaign.

<u>THE STORY</u>:

We begin with Jim, a cab driver, on the job. Several quick cuts of Jim with three different kinds of passengers are shown: (1) a heavier woman, or woman loaded down with packages; (2) a bunch of executives trying to hold a meeting; and (3) a tourist couple. Though we see all these passengers, Jim is given main focus.

A neon "Turn it loose!" graphic serves as the transition from work to play.

After work, Jim parties at a nearby campground. He's the one who actually brings the party because his van is equipped with all the essentials -- beer, food, stereo and big speakers. Since Jim is active, he's got lots of friends. They all pile out of the van and the fun begins.

Jim hooks up with a good-looking woman, Sherry. Everyone has a good time, putting up the tent and grooving to the music. One of Jim's friends, Sam, is a camper who confines his fun to the van where he can watch TV and drink beer. An elderly couple are surprised by the sudden party, but later join in themselves. Jim has one buddy, Moose, who is never seen without a bag of chips and a beer. At the end of the spot, the tent collapses on Moose. He turns on a flashlight and emerges from the tent with the chips and beer intact. Jim, and everyone else, gets a good laugh out of this.

<u>MOOD</u>:

Loads of fun. Energetic and crazy. High-spirited. The definitive good time.

<u>CAST</u>:

The most important member of the cast is Jim, the cab driver.

<u>Jim</u>   - 30-ish, rugged good looks, active. Athletic build, great sense of humor.

<u>Sherry</u> - 25-30-years-old. Good-looking. A great match for Jim. Great figure, great personality. Possibly outdoorsy.

<u>Moose</u> - Minor character. Football player type. Consumes massive quantities of food and beer. "Animal House" was his favorite movie.

Sam   — Minor character. A sedentary type of guy. His idea of a
          good time is watching "Laverne and Shirley" with a 6-pack
          at arm's reach.

Elderly couple — Everyone's grandma and grandpa.

Jim's friends — A group of about 4-6 guys and girls, who love a
               good time.

SETTING:

The opening work situation takes place in and out of a taxi cab. The
cab doesn't have to be in a big city. It can be in a typical American
city.

The campground can be a nearby field, a national park, or a state park.
We're open to suggestions from the director and production company
as to the type of camp site to be used.

TECHNIQUE:

The opening 5 seconds of the spot require a special technique. We want
to cover it with a still camera. From this, we'll get a rapid series
of quick cuts of Jim at work in his cab. We'd like to do this in addition to shooting the opening scenes in motion. In the edit, we'll do
what works best in terms of editing stills and/or live-action film.

Assignment 10-1: Background Data

THE CLIENT: Campbell Soup Co.

THE PRODUCT: V-8 Cocktail vegetable juice is a canned red juice consisting of eight different natural vegetable juices: tomato, carrot, celery, parsley, beets, spinach, watercress, and lettuce. The blend is approximately 70% tomato juice and 30% other juices.

THE MARKET: According to a survey report, one out of five people sampled used V-8 on a regular basis. The product is used as a breakfast drink; for lunch, dinner, and snacks; as a cocktail ingredient; and in soups. V-8 is currently positioned in the red juice/vegetable juice market, which is about three-fourths tomato juice and one-fourth vegetable juice. The principal users and nonusers of V-8 are as follows. A disproportionate amount of vegetable juice is consumed by the 50+ age group. These users account for 57% of consumption. Use of V-8 is very low among the younger age groups, especially the 18–24-year-old segment. It appears that there is a great potential for sales of the product to college students.

THE PACKAGE: Presently, V-8 is packed in four can sizes: 6, 12, 24, and 46 ounces. In addition, a 6-ounce "sleeve pack" (six units per pack) has been marketed with some degree of success.

DISTRIBUTION: V-8 is distributed primarily in retail grocery and food stores. Some 12-ounce cans are available in vending machines.

PRICE: The product is priced slightly higher than tomato juice.

AD BUDGET: $1,000,000.

MARKETING PROBLEM: To get people 18–35 to drink more V-8 more often.

1. Write a script for a 30-second slice-of-life commercial.
2. Write a 30-second comparison commercial in any format.

TELEVISION SCRIPT SHEET

Student name: Advertiser:

Date submitted: Product:

Commercial length: Format:

VIDEO   AUDIO

TELEVISION SCRIPT SHEET

Student name: Advertiser:

Date submitted: Product:

Commercial length: Format:

VIDEO	AUDIO

Assignment 10-2: Background Data

THE CLIENT: Farmer's Friend, Inc.

THE PRODUCT: Viravac is an insoluble herbicide that is mixed into the top two or three inches of soil, where 90% of the weed seeds germinate. The farmer may use his own disc or field cultivator to apply the herbicide. Viravac does not need rain to make it work. It stays put because it attaches itself to the surface of soil particles and organic matter. This is a great advantage over other herbicides, which are less absorptive. Other advantages: Viravac goes to work immediately to kill susceptible germinating grass, and it keeps working even in heavy rain. It gives long-lasting weed control all summer long, the result of which is a cleaner field with a faster, earlier harvest.

THE MARKET: Viravac is used primarily by soybean, cotton, and sunflower farmers, especially in dry climates.

THE PACKAGE: The product is sold in 80-pound bags. "Viravac" is printed in three-inch letters across the top third of the front, and directions for application are given in small print on the bottom two-thirds. Chemical contents are printed on the back.

DISTRIBUTION: Viravac is sold in the South and Midwest at farm supply stores.

PRICE: Although Viravac is slightly more expensive than other herbicides, it requires less product per acre.

AD BUDGET: $50,000 annually.

MARKETING PROBLEM: Nonusers of Viravac think it is too expensive and therefore use competitive products.

1. Write a script for a 60-second demonstration commercial for regional broadcast.
2. Write a 30-second testimonial.

TELEVISION SCRIPT SHEET

Student name: Advertiser:

Date submitted: Product:

Commercial length: Format:

VIDEO   AUDIO

TELEVISION SCRIPT SHEET

Student name: Advertiser:

Date submitted: Product:

Commercial length: Format:

VIDEO   AUDIO

TELEVISION SCRIPT SHEET

Student name: Advertiser:

Date submitted: Product:

Commercial length: Format:

VIDEO	AUDIO

Assignment 10-3: Background Data

THE CLIENT: Carson Cosmetics, Inc.

THE PRODUCT: Silk 'n Soft is a revolutionary therapeutic hand lotion that actually works with the chemistry of the skin to soften, protect, and heal, as no other lotion can. It moisturizes the top layers of the skin at once and stays on the skin longer, even when exposed to water. The white, creamy lotion has a light, herbal fragrance.

THE MARKET: Potential buyers are women aged 24 and up, mainly homemakers.

THE PACKAGE: The product is sold in a 16-ounce, gray plastic squeeze bottle with a matching dispenser top. A four-color photo of a woman's hands is set in the middle of the front of the bottle. The burgundy words "SILK 'N SOFT" are printed in a semicircle over the hands.

DISTRIBUTION: Silk 'n Soft will be sold in national chain and independent drug stores and in the health and beauty departments of discount and grocery stores.

PRICE: $4.25 per bottle, about 50 higher than other therapeutic lotions.

AD BUDGET: $1,000,000 for national rollout.

MARKETING PROBLEM: Other cosmetics with better-known brand names have captured the "lion's share" of the therapeutic hand lotion market.

1. Prepare a storyboard for a 60-second problem-solution commercial.
2. Prepare a 30-second spokesman commercial with music.

TV STORYBOARD FORM

Student name: Advertiser:

Date submitted: Product:

Commercial length: Format:

VIDEO

AUDIO

VIDEO

AUDIO

VIDEO

AUDIO

TV STORYBOARD FORM

Student name: Advertiser:

Date submitted: Product:

Commercial length: Format:

VIDEO

AUDIO

VIDEO

AUDIO

VIDEO

AUDIO

TELEVISION SCRIPT SHEET

Student name: Advertiser:

Date submitted: Product:

Commercial length: Format:

VIDEO   AUDIO

Assignment 10-4: Background Data

THE CLIENT: The Gateway

THE PRODUCT: The Gateway, a well-established and respected department store, is running a special back-to-school promotion. The sale features a nationally known typewriter—a portable electric with a cartridge ribbon system for quick and easy change. It has keyboard controls, repeating action, and either pica or elite type. Six extra cartridges will be given away with every typewriter purchased within one week of the announcement.

THE MARKET: The promotion is aimed at high-school and college students in the metropolitan Denver area.

THE PACKAGE: The typewriter comes in Aegean Blue, Coppertone, and Norwegian Gray. A durable case is included. Black, colored (red, blue, green, brown), and correcting ribbons are available in either nylon or film.

DISTRIBUTION: The sale will be held at all Gateway outlets, including one downtown and three suburban stores.

PRICE: $255.95.

AD BUDGET: $5,000 for this promotion.

MARKETING PROBLEM: To run a successful sale on a very modest budget.

1. Prepare a storyboard for a 30-second spot using a spokesperson.
2. Prepare a 30-second commercial in the product-alone format.

TV STORYBOARD FORM

Student name: Advertiser:

Date submitted: Product:

Commercial length: Format:

VIDEO

AUDIO

VIDEO

AUDIO

VIDEO

AUDIO

TV STORYBOARD FORM

Student name: Advertiser:

Date submitted: Product:

Commercial length: Format:

VIDEO

AUDIO

VIDEO

AUDIO

VIDEO

AUDIO

TELEVISION SCRIPT SHEET

Student name: Advertiser:

Date submitted: Product:

Commercial length: Format:

VIDEO	AUDIO

Assignment 10-5: Marketing Objectives

MARKETING: Sony, the world's largest manufacturer of home electronics equipment, wishes to (1) reach a greater number of potential buyers through the medium of primetime television; (2) encourage dealers and distributors to carry the full line of company products; and (3) increase the public's awareness of the company as a total home electronics manufacturer.

ADVERTISING: The television campaign should (1) show Sony as a manufacturer of a full range of home electronics products—including color TV, black and white TV, clock radios, stereo systems, tape recorders, walk-along radios, and VCRs; (2) support and enhance the company's quality image through pride of ownership; and (3) continue to present company products in a human setting.

1. Write a script for a 60-second slice-of-life commercial.
2. Write a 30-second spinoff.

TELEVISION SCRIPT SHEET

Student name: Advertiser:

Date submitted: Product:

Commercial length: Format:

| VIDEO | AUDIO |

TELEVISION SCRIPT SHEET

Student name: Advertiser:

Date submitted: Product:

Commercial length: Format:

VIDEO	AUDIO

TELEVISION SCRIPT SHEET

Student name: Advertiser:

Date submitted: Product:

Commercial length: Format:

VIDEO	AUDIO

Assignment 10-6: Marketing Objectives

MARKETING: Research shows that "prior experience with the brand" and "advice of a friend or relative" are two of the strongest influences on consumer preferences among house paints. Glidden, a major manufacturer of interior and exterior house paint, believes that a candid-camera testimonial campaign would exploit these research findings.

ADVERTISING: The advertising agency agrees to use a hidden-camera technique in an interview with a real user. The campaign has three objectives: (1) to show customer satisfaction with the quality of Glidden's product by emphasizing particular attributes; (2) to demonstrate the strong brand loyalty among company product users; and (3) to create believability.

1. Prepare a storyboard for a 60-second testimonial spot.
2. Prepare a 30-second spinoff.

TV STORYBOARD FORM

Student name: Advertiser:

Date submitted: Product:

Commercial length: Format:

VIDEO

AUDIO

VIDEO

AUDIO

VIDEO

AUDIO

TV STORYBOARD FORM

Student name: Advertiser:

Date submitted: Product:

Commercial length: Format:

VIDEO

AUDIO

VIDEO

AUDIO

VIDEO

AUDIO

TV STORYBOARD FORM

Student name: Advertiser:

Date submitted: Product:

Commercial length: Format:

VIDEO

AUDIO

VIDEO

AUDIO

VIDEO

AUDIO

Assignment 10-7: Fact Sheet

The following fact sheet should be used in the writing assignments given below. The advertiser is the Australian Trade Commission.

Products: Australian apples and pears

1. A fresh supply of Australian apples and pears has just arrived.

2. Two varieties of pears are Bosc and Parkhams (Park-ums).

3. Both are sweet and succulent and have a distinctive taste.

4. They may look like domestic pears, but their taste is superior—their flesh is white and aromatic.

5. Pears shipped to the U.S. are the best of a vintage crop.

6. The apples are called ''Granny Smith'' apples.

7. Green in color, they are nevertheless magnificent eating apples.

8. These apples can also be used in cooking.

9. Now available in grocery stores and supermarkets at a price about the same as domestic apples and pears.

10. More and more people are asking for them, so hurry—before they are sold out.

1. Write a script for a 30-second commercial in the product-alone format.
2. Write a 30-second spot in any format.

TELEVISION SCRIPT SHEET

Student name: Advertiser:

Date submitted: Product:

Commercial length: Format:

VIDEO	AUDIO

TELEVISION SCRIPT SHEET

Student name: Advertiser:

Date submitted: Product:

Commercial length: Format:

VIDEO   AUDIO

TELEVISION SCRIPT SHEET

Student name: Advertiser:

Date submitted: Product:

Commercial length: Format:

VIDEO   AUDIO

Assignment 10-8: Rewrite

The following radio script begins and ends with an appeal to "looking good." It also emphasizes that savings come from low prices and good service. The two-pronged sales pitch, spiced up with a special offer, is neatly wrapped up in a memorable rhyme that serves as the company's slogan. Make up a name for the company and revise the spot for TV according to the directions given below.

1. Write a script for a 60-second revision of this commercial as a TV demonstration.
2. Write a 30-second television spot in any format.

ANNCR: "Look sharp and you feel sharp." That's
                an old saying that still goes at (ADVERTISER).
                They know that a freshly pressed shirt and
                a spotlessly clean suit can make a real dif-
                ference in the way you feel--and the way you
                come across. You can count on (ADVERTISER) for
                professional laundering and dry cleaning...and
                at prices that may surprise you. Shirts washed
                and pressed, only (PRICE) each. Suits or sport-
                coats dry cleaned, just (PRICE); slacks, (PRICE)
                each. Bulk laundry, sorted, washed and folded,
                (PRICE). (ADVERTISER) uses the most modern
                equipment and the safest techniques to take
                good care of your laundry and dry cleaning.
                Clothes are a big investment, and having your
                clothes professionally dry cleaned will help
                them last longer. So check the closet and the
                clothes hamper, then stop in at (ADVERTISER),
                (LOCATION), on the way to work or home tomorrow.
                Mention (STATION) and you'll also qualify for
                an additional (___%) off any of our services.
                (ADVERTISER). Where the best dressed take their
                cleaning for less.

TELEVISION SCRIPT SHEET

Student name: Advertiser:

Date submitted: Product:

Commercial length: Format:

VIDEO   AUDIO

TELEVISION SCRIPT SHEET

Student name: Advertiser:

Date submitted: Product:

Commercial length: Format:

VIDEO   AUDIO

TELEVISION SCRIPT SHEET

Student name: Advertiser:

Date submitted: Product:

Commercial length: Format:

| VIDEO | AUDIO |

Assignment 10-9: Rewrite

The following commercial for Pan American World Airways uses a tune that is pleasant to hear and easy to sing or hum along with. The listener is called on to "open up" and "look around," which should lead him to think of all the places he hasn't seen. The announcer continues the friendly approach by offering to supply information about Pan Am's service. Read the radio script with careful attention to its overall theme and the specific information it provides. Then rewrite it, as directed below.

1. Prepare a storyboard for this 30-second radio musical.
2. Prepare a storyboard in another format.

MUSIC:	SMALL ENSEMBLE, UPBEAT TEMPO
VOCAL GROUP:	OPEN YOUR EYES! HEY, LOOK AROUND YOU.
	THERE'S A LOT OF WORLD YOU'VE NEVER SEEN.
MUSIC:	CONTINUE UNDER
ANNCR:	There's one airline that can help you change all that. Pan Am. America's airline to the world. To sixty-one countries on all six continents. Anytime you feel you've been waiting around ... long enough.
VOCAL GROUP:	WELCOME TO OUR WORLD.
	WELCOME TO OUR WORLD.
	WELCOME TO THE WORLD OF PAN AM.
	AMERICA'S AIRLINE TO THE WORLD.
ANNCR (LIVE, LOCAL, OVER MUSIC):	Going to London or Amsterdam? Pan Am can take you there from Philadelphia three times a week. Just take Airflight to Pan Am's Worldport where you can make connections to Pan Am's 747 to London or Amsterdam. Call your travel agent for reservations.

TV STORYBOARD FORM

Student name: Advertiser:

Date submitted: Product:

Commercial length: Format:

VIDEO

AUDIO

VIDEO

AUDIO

VIDEO

AUDIO

TV STORYBOARD FORM

Student name: Advertiser:

Date submitted: Product:

Commercial length: Format:

VIDEO

AUDIO

VIDEO

AUDIO

VIDEO

AUDIO

TV STORYBOARD FORM

Student name: Advertiser:

Date submitted: Product:

Commercial length: Format:

VIDEO

AUDIO

VIDEO

AUDIO

VIDEO

AUDIO

Assignment 10-10: Rewrite

This television script was based on the marketing and advertising objectives for Prudential Property and Casualty Insurance Co. given in Chapter 7. Revise it according to the directions below.

1. Using the same format, write a script for a 30-second version of this 60-second commercial.
2. Rewrite the spot in a different 60-second format.

MUSIC:	UNDER: SFX UNDER _
MAN: (ANSWERING PHONE IN OFFICE):	Hi, honey. What's new?
WOMAN: (CALLING FROM HOME)	Well, the fire's out.
MAN:	Fire?
WOMAN (IN BURNED-OUT KITCHEN):	We'll have to redo the kitchen....But they're coming for the car.
MAN:	What car?
WOMAN (SHOT OF WRECKED CAR):	Our car.
MAN:	Honey...
WOMAN (WAVING TO PLUMBER):	But at least the plumber's ankle is okay.
MAN:	The plumber's ankle?
WOMAN:	Yeah. He was fixing the faucet when the fire broke out.
MAN:	Honey...honey, call...call Prudential.
WOMAN:	Life insurance?
ANNCR (V.O.):	Now a Prudential agent can provide insurance for your car and home. Same Prudential planning and service.
WOMAN:	It's all taken care of.
ANNCR (V.O.):	Most claims are settled with a phone call. And some people even save money by changing to Prudential for Car and Homeowner's Insurance.
WOMAN:	It's nice to save money.
MAN (WHO HAS ARRIVED HOME):	With someone you know.
WOMAN:	By the way, guess who bit the mailman.
CHORUS (SUPER LOGO AND NAME):	Get a piece of the rock.
ANNCR (SUPER NAME AND "LIFE-HEALTH-AUTO-HOME"):	Prudential Insurance.
MUSIC:	OUT

TELEVISION SCRIPT SHEET

Student name: Advertiser:

Date submitted: Product:

Commercial length: Format:

VIDEO	AUDIO

TELEVISION SCRIPT SHEET

Student name: Advertiser:

Date submitted: Product:

Commercial length: Format:

| VIDEO | AUDIO |

TELEVISION SCRIPT SHEET

Student name: Advertiser:

Date submitted: Product:

Commercial length: Format:

VIDEO	AUDIO

Assignment 10-11: Rewrite

The print ad below appeared with a photograph of a moving Volvo Turbo as viewed from behind. Examine the copy and then write a television commercial based on the same selling idea.

1. Write a script for a 60-second commercial in the narrative format.
2. Write a 30-second comparison spot.

THE VOLVO TURBO AS MOST COMMONLY VIEWED FROM A BMW 318i.

The posterior of a Volvo Turbo may not be its most attractive feature, but it's the one BMW 318i owners will be seeing a lot of.

In an independent test* of 0 to 60 acceleration, the intercooled Turbo from Volvo beat the 318i by almost two seconds.

Results like this have prompted *Car and Driver* to call the Volvo Turbo "a missile."

And *Road & Track* describes its handling and performance as "Exemplary."

So before you run out and buy the ultimate driving machine, test drive the intercooled Turbo from Volvo.

It could prevent you from becoming one of those BMW owners with 20/20 hindsight.

*Tests of acceleration conducted by *Car and Driver.*

THE TURBO+
By Volvo.

© 1984 VOLVO OF AMERICA CORPORATION

TELEVISION SCRIPT SHEET

Student name: Advertiser:

Date submitted: Product:

Commercial length: Format:

VIDEO	AUDIO

TELEVISION SCRIPT SHEET

Student name: Advertiser:

Date submitted: Product:

Commercial length: Format:

| VIDEO | AUDIO |

TELEVISION SCRIPT SHEET

Student name: Advertiser:

Date submitted: Product:

Commercial length: Format:

VIDEO	AUDIO

Assignment 10-12: Rewrite

The following print ad was accompanied by ''primitive'' drawings of a Perrier bottle cap above and four prehistoric-looking animals below. Study the copy and revise the ad for television as directed.

BORN SALT-FREE.

Prehistoric cuisine was salt-free, of course. If you could manage to make a fire, you were ahead of the game. And if the game was well-done, you were a four-star chef. Because stone-age man didn't know there was such a thing as salt. Or high-blood pressure, either.

And his favorite libation came from a pure, sparkling, naturally salt-free spring. The spring we now call Perrier. Earth's first soft drink.

Today, modern man is over-salted. He salts his peas, his porterhouse, his peanuts. Most of his soft drinks, even the diet drinks, are salted, too.

Not Perrier. Perrier has been salt-free since the day it was born. And while other beverages have had to change their contents, the only thing we've had to change is our label. Just to let you know.

Perrier. Earth's First Soft Drink.™

1. Prepare a storyboard for a 30-second spot in the slice-of-life format using fantasy.
2. Prepare a 30-second commercial in any format.

TV STORYBOARD FORM

Student name: Advertiser:

Date submitted: Product:

Commercial length: Format:

VIDEO

AUDIO

VIDEO

AUDIO

VIDEO

AUDIO

TV STORYBOARD FORM

Student name: Advertiser:

Date submitted: Product:

Commercial length: Format:

VIDEO

AUDIO

VIDEO

AUDIO

VIDEO

AUDIO

TELEVISION SCRIPT SHEET

Student name: Advertiser:

Date submitted: Product:

Commercial length: Format:

VIDEO	AUDIO

Section Four:
Broadcast Considerations

Testing The Commercial 11

By Patrick J. Kelly
Marketing Research Associates

The objective of any TV commercial testing service is to measure the ability of the commercial to sell, to be remembered, and to communicate. The need to know is accentuated by the size of the advertising budget invested in a campaign. With such a sizable investment at stake, it is advisable to know, beforehand, how a specific commercial will perform compared with another, either for the same product or for a competitor's product. The effectiveness of commercials varies widely.

To find out just where a specific commercial lies in the effectiveness spectrum, services have been established to uncover this information. Following are brief descriptions of some of the leading testing services—how they operate and what they offer.

Gallup & Robinson, Inc.

Gallup & Robinson's system of television commercial evaluation provides three basic facilities: On-Air Syndicated Total Prime Time Television Research (TPT); On-Air Custom; and Theater Pre-Tests. The survey is based on interviews with approximately 3,300 men and women, 18 years of age and older, selected from telephone directories covering the Philadelphia area.

During the interview, last night's primetime program schedule is read, and the interviewee is asked to reconstruct his viewing pattern by half-hour segments. All viewers are exposed to brand-name cues selected from the viewer's total viewing pattern via a priority system that includes all client commercials, competitive commercials, and the necessary balance from an "all other" group.

Viewers claiming recall of any given commercial are asked a series of open-ended questions. The answers are recorded to determine proof of commercial registration (PCR), level of idea communication and commercial persuasiveness. PCR scores are reported as a percentage of the available audience—men or women exposed to and asked about commercial exposure.

Because of increased participation and increased complexity in the development of TV marketing strategies, some advertisers need tailor-made measurements. In response to this need, Gallup & Robinson has developed a measurement on individual programs whenever, wherever, and with whomever the advertiser pleases.

The On-Air Single Show Surveys provide delayed, aided recall measurements using telephone interviewing. The service is available in 24 areas across the country, and additional markets can be added if needed. The basic reports developed are Proved Commercial Registration (PCR) and verbatim playback profiles leading to data on idea communication and buying attitudes.

For advertisers who want to pretest commercials, an in-theater testing arrangement is available. A sample of respondents is invited to attend a theater to view a TV program. After viewing the program, they are questioned about the program and television in general— nothing is said about the commercial spliced into the film. The day following exposure, the respondents are interviewed by telephone to obtain recall levels and idea communication and favorable buying attitude effectiveness data.

Burke Marketing Research, Inc.

The Standard Burke Technique involves telephone interviews the day after the commercial was aired, using the aided recall method and reflecting normal in-the-home viewing situations.

The usual sample size is 200 viewers of the test program, which yields a Commercial Audience (those who were actually in the room with the set, not asleep and not changing channels at the time of the test commercial exposure) of approximately 150, varying slightly in either direction, depending on the type of program. Tests using other sample sizes can be arranged.

Respondents are those who claim to have watched the program on which the test commercial was telecast. Interviewing times are flexible, so that the interviewers can best reach the particular audience segment desired.

The following timetable is standard for most Burke day-after recall tests:

Flash scores, claimed and related recall, percentaged on Commercial Audience, are reported by telephone during the morning of the day following the test. These rapidly computed scores are usually accurate within one or two percentage points, but are confirmed within about three more days. Friday, Saturday, and Sunday tests are flash-reported on the following Monday.

One hundred percent of the related and unrelated verbatims, coded and uncoded, can be available about five days after the date of interviewing. Final reports are available between three and four weeks from date of interviewing.

The standard report contains, basically, three items of decision-making information:

1. A quantitative measure of the communication's effectiveness
2. A coded and categorized summary of all that was remembered about the commercial
3. A verbatim transcription of the playback from every respondent recalling anything about the commercial

Additionally, Burke maintains a file of normative data against which recall scores for a specific study may be compared. Current normative data show mean averages, ranges, and bar graph distributions of claimed and related scores by length of commercial, product category, and sex.

Schwerin Research Corp.

Central to the Schwerin Research Corp. system is the assumption that advertising's ability to persuade consumers to prefer a given brand over its competition is the key indicator of effectiveness. Based on this assumption, several measures have been developed to reflect this position.

The Standard Service includes the Competitive Preference Score, Persuasibility Index, Brand Identification (Unaided), and Unaided Recall and Involvement. To supplement the basic standard measure, Schwerin Research has developed a variety of "diagnostic" measurements that are used to assist in understanding the influence underlying advertising effectiveness—the Extended Service.

The technique used by Schwerin to measure the effectiveness of television advertising centers on a test audience in a test theater. A randomly selected panel is subjected to viewing a "pilot" TV film throughout which are interspersed some TV commercials.

The test audience is selected from telephone directories covering the geographical area surrounding a particular test center. Although the total audience on a given night represents a cross-section of the population 16 years of age or older and test data are obtained from the entire audience, the sample may be redefined after the fact so that test results for a particular product

are based only on relevant consumers—namely, the analytical sample.

Following the introductory warm-up during which the test director outlines the purpose of the session and gives specific procedural instructions—but before any exposure to a stimulus of any kind has taken place—the audience is offered the chance to win some prizes. In order to qualify for a prize, every respondent is asked to complete a ballot by checking the particular brand of which he would like to receive a quantity as a prize. Several product categories are included, and within each are listed the principal competing brands. Tickets are drawn on stage and the winner is given a specified amount of the product he selected in a given category. This technique may be regarded as a simulation of real buying behavior and ultimately provides data for the "Pre-Choice Measurement."

The audience is then shown the pilot program and three commercials (for one of the brands in each of the "Pre-Choice" checklists). The same pilot program is repeated from session to session to eliminate this element as a variable.

At the conclusion of the program, measures of "Unaided Recall" and "Brand Identification" are obtained, followed by the "Post-Choice Measurement," which is developed in the same manner as the "Pre-Choice" brand selections and drawings.

Summarization of the brand selections made after exposure to the test advertisement provides data for the "Post-Choice" percentages, which reflect the proportions of consumers favorably disposed toward brands in the respective product fields after exposure to a commercial for a brand in that field. The "Post-Choice" information serves as the final ingredient for the overall effectiveness measure.

Next, the involvement measure is obtained, followed by a short audience discussion about the program. For Extended Service Tests, the advertisement is again shown—out of program context—allowing for the special diagnostic questioning.

AdTel, Ltd.

The AdTel technique uses a dual-cable CATV system and two balanced purchase diary panels of 1,200 households each. The system has been wired using two cables, thus permitting wiring of panel homes to either cable to provide an alternate A and B checkerboard distribution.

AdTel can cut in test commercials to the B homes, while the A homes continue to get normal ad exposure. The corporate client must own the time—network or spot—into which the test commercial is cut. A client can have an unlimited number of cut-ins made without paying any cut-in charge.

Two matched panels are maintained—one for each cable. Panel families are personally recruited and trained. They must record all their food, drug, and other appropriate purchases in a weekly diary.

In addition to purchase information, the diary contains a symptom section that enables AdTel to measure low-incidence health care products based on usage. A household reports the number of times each brand was taken by family members for various symptoms—headache, stomach ache, cold, cough, etc. This information makes it possible for a manufacturer to test a campaign against a specific usage.

Panel members receive points for completing their weekly diaries. These points are redeemable for merchandise from a well-known mail-order catalog. These, together with other incentives, total about $100 a year for the consistent but average housewife.

To substantiate the written reports, AdTel conducts quarterly pantry and medicine chest audits. These records are compared by computer against diary-reported purchases. This follow-up check helps to impress panelists that AdTel wants complete and accurate diary entries.

Data from the purchase diaries are processed into a four-week report. For each brand specified by the client, shares of unduplicated families purchasing, units, dollars, volume in ounces or another common denominator, and percentage of deal volume are shown.

In addition, a client receives a raw deck of data cards (or tape) covering every diary-recorded transaction in the product categories desired. These data enable the client to track such factors as trial and repeat, brand switching, the demographics of triers, users, and switchers, the importance of dealing, etc.

AdTel also conducts three attitude and awareness studies throughout the year among people on the cable but not on the panel. These studies are intended to be diagnostic rather than definitive and can be helpful in guiding analysis of the diary panel data.

Milwaukee Advertising Laboratory

The Milwaukee Advertising Laboratory is a research facility that provides a set of controlled conditions in a natural setting, within which the sales effectiveness of newspaper, Sunday supplement, direct mail, and television advertising can be measured without disturbing a current marketing program.

Two matched markets were developed by taking the four counties comprising the Greater Milwaukee Market and dividing them into 104 newspaper circulation districts with about 2,500 newspaper subscribers in each. These were then split into two equal and matched markets of 52 districts each. From these two markets, probability samples of 750 families each are drawn.

Newspaper advertising reaching these two matching markets is controlled on a split-run and split distribution basis. Television advertising is controlled through the use of an electronic muter installed in all of the TV sets of the two samples. With the muter in use, it is possible to blank out a set of commercials from one group, while the other group receives the message. The television set simply goes blank, as does the sound, for the interim of the commercial but then returns to "live" for the program.

To collect the needed information, the Laboratory makes use of a consumer purchase diary. Each homemaker in each sample is asked to send in a weekly diary of all branded merchandise bought during the week. She is given instructions on how to do this during a basic placement interview.

To compensate the homemaker for her cooperation, the Laboratory provides free maintenance service on all TV sets in the household for the duration of the householder's participation as a panel member. Also, she can earn merchandise prizes from points earned by continued cooperation.

The weekly diaries are processed by computer, and printouts are sent directly to subscribing advertisers and their agencies. The reports show the total number of units bought in the product category, the distribution of brand shares by units, and the percentage in each market separately. Parallel reports cover dollar sales in total and by brand, the volume of sales in total and by brand, and additional data on the extent to which dealing affects volume each month.

Commercial Testing Service

Two types of measurements to appraise the performance of television commercials are offered by Commercial Testing Service: an evaluative measure and a diagnostic measure.

The evaluative measures are related to how well the commercial succeeds in building consumer acceptance and interest in the advertised brand. In addition to the overall measure of the effectiveness, CTS also offers measures defined by demographic characteristics (age, education, etc.), by product usage characteristics (heavy versus light users), and by brand attitude or brand usage segments.

The diagnostic measures are designed to appraise the content and execution of the commercial, including analysis of the points communicated and the extent to which the commercial message is considered important, believable, interesting, or involving.

Invitations to serve on a panel are mailed to residents living within a four- to six-mile radius of a suburban theater in which the research session will be held. The invitation offers an opportunity to express opinions on television programs and commercials and states that door prizes will be awarded along with additional incentives for attendance and cooperation.

The testing procedure is as follows: Respondents are given a questionnaire in which they rate a number of brands in a number of product categories, using a five-point attitude scale. They are then shown a film that they are told is being considered for TV. Within the film are four commercials for noncompeting brands in some but not all of the product categories for which the respondents had previously indicated brand ratings. After the screening, they are given a second questionnaire with several questions about the film. Then they are told that there will be a series of drawings and that the prizes will be a specified number of units of the product. They are asked to indicate how many of each of a restricted list of competitive brands they would like to win if their name is drawn. Obviously, the respondent would tend to indicate more of the brand most preferred.

A third questionnaire contains, for each commercial, a number of open-ended questions designed to provide information used in the diagnostic tabulation. It is also possible to include questions of the client's own design in this questionnaire.

The principal measure provided shows the gain or loss in buying interest caused by advertising exposure. Respondent attitude toward the various brands is predicated on the number of each brand indicated in the prize-drawing procedure. This ranking compared with the attitude recorded prior to test advertising indicates the effectiveness of the commercial.

Producing The Commercial 12

You've done the research. You've come up with the right concept and you've written a taut, tight script with a strong selling idea. Approval within the agency and from the client has been obtained, and the budget has been okayed. This is the go-ahead sign for production, and this is the signal for the producer to take over.

Ideally, you have worked closely with the producer in the creation of the commercial. During this time, he has assisted and guided you with his imagination and technical expertise. From now on, he is in charge, and you will assist and guide him.

The Producer's Role

Some producers work for production firms; some are strictly free-lance. For our example, let's assume the producer is on staff at the agency. What does he do?

First, we should assume that the producer really knows the ins and out of radio, film, tape, and live media. Completely. Given that knowledge as a base, he works from two points of view: creative and practical. He contributes his creativity to help bring about an imaginative, professional, selling message. At the same time, he works within the production budget, keeps production moving ahead, and is the hub around which a dozen or more phases of commercial making are like the spokes of a wheel. He combines his artistic and business sense under one hat, because only a combination of these polarized talents will help make an effective commercial.

Even though the expense of producing a radio commercial is a fraction of the cost of a TV commercial, the same care, creativity, and professionalism must be devoted to it. The same basic principles and concerns that apply to TV production apply to radio, with possibly one major exception: Radio production is rarely given over to "outside" production houses. Therefore, there is no bidding system.

The agency producer normally handles every detail, such as the booking of a studio, the hiring of a qualified sound engineer and a sound effects man, casting, the quality reproduction of the "master" tape, etc. Usually, however, when a jingle or original music is re-

quired, the agency hires an outside contractor who handles the creation and production of the jingle/music, reporting to the agency producer. Although the rest of this chapter deals specifically with TV production, you should be aware that the same guidelines and virtually the same steps apply to radio production.

Producing for TV

After the commercial is finally approved, the television producer has several copies of the storyboard made. He sends these for bids to production houses, which have been selected from a long list as best qualified for this particular type of commercial. The number of bids varies. Some agencies and clients insist on as many as five bids. Others settle for three. Still others, having had an agreeable experience with a particular firm's work in the past, may opt for that house—if the price is right.

Production houses can generalize or specialize. Animation may be one firm's forte; unusual type-photography may be another's; and sensitivity toward talent may be another's. The producer takes this into consideration when he sends the storyboard out for bids. He also considers each firm's past performance, directors on staff, current output, adherence to shooting schedules, production talent, and ability to deliver on time. And, of course, he considers the price.

When the selection has been made, a contract is drawn up between the agency (acting in behalf of the client) and the production house. Nothing is left to chance or to memory. A commercial represents a big investment for the client, and production costs go up each year. In the past ten years, the increase ranges from 150 to 200 percent.

Preproduction Meeting

Businessmen seem to find all kinds of excuses for holding meetings, but there is a good reason for the preproduction conference: It is a meeting of minds. It is attended by the production house representatives (including its producer and director, if possible), the writer, and the art director. It is chaired by the agency producer. Some clients attend in order to be reassured that their objectives are being met.

At this meeting, the storyboard is reviewed frame by frame, sequence by sequence. The objective is kept clearly in mind, and all suggestions and refinements are focused on meeting it. Ideas are exchanged on sets, actors, sound effects, music—every facet of the spot. Agreement and understanding are reached, a shooting schedule is planned, and the production house goes to work. It sets aside studio time for the shooting and arranges for the crew. If locations are indicated in the storyboard, the house arranges for a scouting date—one the agency producer can make.

From this meeting on, the agency producer is in day-to-day contact with the production firm. The details are multitudinous. Sets must be designed, and the sketches must be approved. Props are gathered, ordered, or built. Costumes are agreed on. The director selects his cameraman; art work and titles are executed and approved. Not even the smallest detail should go unplanned.

Auditions are held for actors and announcers. (The casting procedure is examined at length later in this chapter.)

The producer will take your finished and approved script and list everything needed. He'll have a conference with the TV station's production manager as well as the show's producer and director. (At smaller TV stations, these may be one and the same person.) Once the talent is cast, the props gathered, and the art work completed, rehearsal time is set up. This usually takes place immediately prior to the actual show.

Shooting Date

Your commercial is to be shot on a studio sound stage. Unfortunately, last-minute preparation is the rule rather than the exception. Final touches are given to the set, and the property master arranges the props (including duplicates and triplicates, in case of breakage or soilage).

The agency producer is the voice of authority on the set. He works closely with the production house team, constantly consulting with director, cameraman, and crew chiefs. Lighting is set for the first scene. Actors rehearse, get their makeup, rehearse some more. And after much coffee and prune danish, the assistant director calls for quiet on the set, and the director goes for Take One, Scene One.

Because time in the studio is so valuable, your producer and the show's director will work fast. Camera moves will be plotted and written on the script. (Station directors seem to prefer this practice to the use of storyboards, although they will consult your board and often make suggestions.) Everyone involved learns his commercial cues. The technical director (responsible for picture quality), the sound engineer, the cameraman, the floor manager, and the director all work as a team to give your commercial professional smoothness and pace.

As the creator of this commercial, you are in evidence. You observe. You comment, but for everyone's sanity you restrict your comments to one person—the agency producer, the man or woman in charge. He or she will relay your observations and suggestions to the director. You may wonder if a piece of business may be acted differently to get a better effect. You may question an on-camera reading or prefer a tighter close-up of the product than the director has set up. The more you learn about production, the more valuable your suggestions will become, and, consequently, the more experience you will bring to your next creative assignment.

Take follows take, scene follows scene. Often, the pace seems snail-like, but professionalism includes a large dose of patience. Use it. And finally, after a good take on the last scene, the shooting portion of this production is wrapped up.

Sound & Music

Your commercial may require that the sound track be recorded simultaneously with the shooting, especially if actors are involved in a problem-solution structure. Or, if your commercial calls for an announcer voice-over, chances are good that the producer will tape the audio track before the studio date.

At this taping session, held in a sound studio, the announcer and/or actors work with the script, rehearsing it under the direction of the agency producer. Sound experts monitor the voice levels, adjust microphones for position, and keep a log of the takes. The length of the session depends on the complexity of your commercial and the talents of your announcer and actors. At this session, the writer contributes suggestions as to inflections, emphasis, pacing, etc. He is sometimes asked to rewrite a sequence that may be awkward to read. A writer can often improve a commercial in the recording studio, just as he can at the actual shooting, by constantly being alert to the possibilities of enhancing the commercial's communicability—or, in plain English, by making the persuasion and sell come through.

Music and sound effects may be recorded at this session or at separate sessions. Recording tape gives a producer flexibility. He can record voice, sound effects, or music on separate tracks. If the music has been selected from "stock"—a large bank of music and musical effects that is readily available in large cities—that music is transferred to tape. If musicians and singers are used, this recording session is set up and conducted in a manner similar to the announcer's.

At last, the producer has, say, three tapes: announcer, music, and sound effects. They are transferred to 35mm magnetic tape. The producer then arranges for a mix. At a sound studio with multitrack facilities, the three tapes are placed on separate reels, synchronized for time, and run. The sound engineer "mixes" the tracks together, combines them, each with its own level of volume. The result is a single track with all the sound combined, each at the proper level and intensity.

Going for Approval & After

Being able to juggle might help any producer. Many things have to be done, and all at just about the same time.

If you are filming your commercial, the "dailies" will be available on the day following the shooting date. Dailies are the takes that met on-set approval for printing. Of course, if you are shooting on videotape, your dailies are immediately available for viewing and scene selection.

The producer notes the clack-board number of each preferred take, and these are pulled out of the master reel. Edited together, they become the work print. There are no dissolves or titles in this print. It is for viewing, for reediting work, and for approvals. These latter are obtained at an interlock session; the film is run through one projector, and the sound track is played through another in sync. Additional changes may be suggested. From this point to finish, however, changes are more involved and more costly than they were before.

When approvals are given on the work print, the producer and the film editor pull out the original (and, you hope, still unscratched) footage. In the film laboratory, each sequence is assembled in order and combined with any special-effects footage, titles, etc. Cuts or dissolves are incorporated into the film where directed. The sound track is physically incorporated onto the resultant film, producing the answer print.

Again, approvals are needed. Color or tonal values are checked, and, if found wanting, noted. Smoothness and length of dissolves are also checked. Once again, the lab goes to work and comes out with a corrected answer print. Given its approval, the lab produces the final, correct, perfect release print.

The producer's job is almost over. And so is yours, as creator, at least for this commercial. Prints for on-air use are ordered, received, checked out carefully for quality, and sent to whatever TV stations are on the media schedule.

All the foregoing is, of necessity, but a summary of events in the production life of a TV or radio commercial. Details would fill a book at least the length of this one. But the summary should give you some indication of the enormous attention to detail, as well as the combination of creativity and craftmanship, that so many people expend to make a commercial an effective selling tool.

Production Choices

Producing a commercial today takes much less time than it did a few years ago. Instead of weeks, you can now shoot and finish a film commercial in a few days. This reduction in time has been accomplished by the procedure of transfering negative film to videotape. For example, you can shoot film on Monday, have the film lab develop the negative that night, view dailies Tuesday, and transfer film to tape and edit on Wednesday. By the end of the day, you can have a finished commercial. If you shoot on videotape, completion time can be even shorter. You can start editing immediately after the shoot.

Like production times, production costs vary greatly. But while the time necessary to shoot, process, and edit a TV spot has generally declined, costs have skyrocketed. Today, $300,000 commercials are not at all uncommon. Yet, the majority of spots, even those produced at major production houses, cost considerably less. And, if you are working at a small agency for small-budget clients, you will probably produce commercials for less than $5,000. Exhibits 12-1 and 12-2 show production costs for typical radio and TV commercials. They suggest, if nothing else, that the commercial creator is responsible for making every client dollar do its job. And that job is to sell.

Producing a commercial takes detailed planning.

Exhibit 12-1. Estimated Cost of Producing a 30-Second Radio Commercial—1984

Original music with creative fee (includes studio time, three singers, rhythm section)	$5,000–$7,000
1 hour announcer	175.00
2 hour studio (mix)	150.00
1/4" stock	20.00
1/2" stock	32.00
Dupe master	18.00
1/4" stock (mix)	20.00
10 dubs	10.10
Producer copy	9.00
Total	$434.10

— No Residuals Estimated —

Exhibit 12-2. Estimated Cost of Producing a 30-Second TV Commercial in 35mm Color Film—1984*

Studio Rental $4,700.00

Preparation

Director, assistant director (one day)	2,950.00

Set Preparation

Crew costs (6 days)

Set designer	412.50
Scenic artist	675.00
Stylist	3,500.00
Carpenters	1,500.00
Chief grip	450.00
Second grip	420.00
Chief prop—inside (2 days)	370.00
Chief prop—outside	900.00
Chief electrician (2 days)	500.00
Assistant director	2,150.00
Pension & welfare	2,719.38

Shooting Crew

Producer	2,875.00
Director (staff)	6,000.00
Assistant director	963.00
Script clerk	263.00
Set designer	1,237.50
Cameraman	679.00
Assistant cameraman	488.00
Chief electrician	688.00
Assistant electrician	360.00
Stylist	613.00
Chief grip	600.00
Second grip	563.00
Chief prop	324.00
Second prop	324.00
Sound boom man	219.00
Sound recordist	140.00
Sound mixer	352.00
Makeup artist	625.00
Hairdresser	625.00
Wardrobe	1,514.00
Pension & welfare	4,863.13

Striking

One prop, one electrician, one grip (including pension & welfare)	731.25

Equipment

Camera, lights, sound	5,100.00

Miscellaneous

Insurance, shipping, inspecting, etc.	750.00

Film & Processing   3,282.00

Lettering, Animation, Opticals   1,585.00

Editing

Supervising editor, editor, assistant editor, and projectionist	8,991.00

Re-Recording & Mixing

Sound track—outside	625.00

Subtotal $ 66,626.76

Production House Fee   21,640.00

Production House Total   88,266.76

Talent

Three on-camera	2,580.00
One voice-over (V.O. includes pension & welfare)	610.00

Music

Copy & arrange	5,850.00
Pension & welfare	585.00

Recording

Studio & materials	415.00

Photostats   100.00

Photoscripts   325.00

Production Visuals   2,400.00

Wardrobe   2,000.00

Total Costs $103,131.76

Agency commission (17.65%)   18,202.76

Total $121,334.52

*Costs, given here for New York, Chicago, and Los Angeles, are lower in smaller cities.

Besides deciding how much time you can afford to spend and how much money you can afford to invest in making your commercial, you must answer a number of other important questions. Will you shoot on location or in a studio? Will you use film or videotape? If you choose film, what size will be most effective and least costly? Who will you select to perform, direct, and edit the commercial?

In addition, technical experts can provide you with a vast array of special effects: fancy opticals, wipes, dissolves, overlaps, fractionalized or split-screen units, prism shots, flash cuts, slow and fast motion—the list is almost endless.

You can take and retake sequences and then select the ones best qualified for your commercial. You can zero in with extreme microphotography. You can, as one golf ball spot did, start on a close-up of the ball and zoom back for what seems like half a mile. You can use a narrow field of vision or a wide-angle lens. You can also pan, truck, go out of focus, or come into focus. In the commercials that you create, you are limited only by your knowledge and imagination, your production staff's ingenuity, and, of course, by your client's time and money.

Studio Shooting

Studios in major cities have complete facilities for photographing the most complex commercials. Studios range in size from small ''insert'' rooms used exclusively for close-up work (of packages, hands, labels, etc.) to animation studios in which drawings are photographed frame by frame—to the huge, arena-like sound stages in the Los Angeles, California, area. Most of the latter belong to major feature-film studios, which often devote a large portion of their production schedules to the filming of TV programs and spots.

Reliable, creative production houses either have their own studios or rent space for shooting a commercial. These companies can be found in Canada, Mexico, and Puerto Rico and throughout Europe. Just as Hollywood is no longer the only center for feature films, it and New York City are no longer the only centers for the production of spots for television. Many agencies and clients use European studios for special scenes or special casting, not to mention production economies. Because the production field is extremely competitive, there is practically no limit to the effects you can ask for and get—budget permitting.

There are many good production houses in the smaller cities today. And, if you are working for a small client with a limited production budget, you may very well produce your commercial at the local television station. If this is the case, it is important to realize that you cannot do in Burlington, Iowa, what you might do in Hollywood. Understand the limitations of local low-budget production and plan your commercial accordingly. Keep it simple. Don't try for tricky effects.

Don't think you can find local talent that can pull off an outstanding slice-of-life commercial.

Location Shooting

More and more, commercials are being shot on location. And for many good reasons. Improvement in film quality, fast jet travel, wider use of off-beat camera techniques, and the compelling desire to look different from competition are some. But the overriding reason is authenticity or realism. For many commercials today, this demand practically necessitates location shooting—even multilocation shooting is required in some cases.

For talent, production crew, agency staff, and client personnel to go on location, the budget must be generous and the objectives worthwhile. Location shooting is costly, and it must be weighed against achieving (or trying to achieve) authenticity in a studio. Because of the colorful, authentic locales of feature films, viewers have grown accustomed to realism. And this quality in a commercial can add to the spot's believability.

Commercials for spaghetti are now filmed in Italy, the coffee tree areas of Colombia are familiar TV sights, and Paris is a much-used backdrop for fashion and perfume spots. Airlines with overseas routes enhance their images by spotlighting foreign scenes. Pipe tobacco spots are photographed on ski jumps, and fresh orange juice commercials are shot on Florida beaches. All these locations are used for the realism they bring to the commercials.

As we have stated, motion pictures are, in part, responsible for this trend. Another stimulus has come from the flexibility of TV news programs whose cameramen and reporters are all over the world. On-the-spot reports are filed every day and funneled into every TV home as a matter of course. Again, viewers have come to expect location shots from around the world.

Be guided by your objectives in deciding between studio and location. If location shooting will give you a more authentic-looking commercial for your product, make it show up on your storyboard. Perhaps you need a location only to set the stage for your message. If this is the case, your producer can obtain footage already in existence from a stock film company. Then you can shoot the balance of your commercial in close-ups in a studio—and save. You will also find that sometimes it is cheaper to go on location to get a shot than to build a set in a studio. For example, rather than build a set to show a woman shopping in a supermarket, shoot the scene in the local supermarket.

Live

Early in the game, you must decide whether your commercial will be presented live or prerecorded on film or videotape. In many instances, your spot will have been planned with one of these methods in mind.

Live commercials were the rule in the early days of television, even for network shows. From simplistic announcer-on-camera-holding-the-product to elaborate studio productions, live commercials, telecast as they were being performed, were sometimes exciting, usually frustrating, and often dull.

Every nuance, every light, every piece of business, props, letter-perfect actors—every detail of a live commercial had to be preplanned and rehearsed. The comic history of television includes commercials that featured refrigerator doors that wouldn't open, dogs that refused pet food, cleansers that failed to wipe up dirt. No wonder film became the major medium for commercials!

Relatively few commercials are done live today. And most of these are on news and personality shows of local TV stations. Some network "talk-and-plug-my-latest-movie" shows have the host or announcer deliver the commercial, but these are the exceptions rather than the rule.

Creating a commercial for live delivery demands simplicity, mostly because your set will be restricting. The local station might have only one camera—two, if you're lucky. So you must plan your moves and dissolves and cuts carefully, allowing time for changing a lens or repositioning a camera. And you cannot expect to have carte blanche in sets or lighting or talent. Whatever titles you use may be art work, shown directly on camera, or translated into slides and fed into the system on cue by the director.

Videotape

The proponents of videotape argue that it has three basic advantages over film: a more brilliant and clearer picture, better sound, a shorter production time, and more control in the studio—you can see what you're doing each step of the way.

Most people are unable to distinguish between a live telecast and one on videotape. Tape records electronically and plays back electronically for transmission; there is no perceptible loss of quality. Tape gives commercials a sense of "presence," which can be important to advertisers.

Speed is all-important to advertiser and agency. Tape is immediate because it requires no processing, whereas film must be developed, printed, and copied before it can be edited. A tape commercial can be completed in hours, whereas film can take weeks.

Tape also allows the entire production team to view "takes" immediately, make suggestions and improvements, and retake and view again. Reshooting with film means rerenting studio and equipment and calling back crew and performers.

If you want the viewer to feel that what he is seeing is happening at the time he is seeing it, videotape will work. If it would be incredible to the viewer that what he is seeing is happening as he sees it, you probably do not want the "live" look. And film may be your choice for this reason alone.

Can you shoot videotape and avoid the "live" look? Yes, if you light for film and use filters over the camera lens. So, wanting the "live" look is a reason to use videotape, but the "live" look can be avoided. And if you don't want it, tape can still be considered.

The "live" look works well for an on-camera spokesman commercial. The viewer can accept the idea that the spokesperson is at that moment in a television studio presenting the product story. The "live" look does not work for a slice-of-life commercial. The viewer cannot believe that he is at the moment viewing a family at their breakfast table solving the teenage eating problem with a particular brand of cereal. He will accept this contrivance in a little filmed drama. But if it looks "live," he will reject it as implausible.

Can the viewer believe that what he is seeing could be happening as he sees it? This is the basic question you should ask in order to determine if you want the "live" look. If appropriate, the "live" look is powerful. We take a particular interest in seeing what is happening right now.

Film

The proponents of film talk primarily about the beauty of the "film look." And there is little doubt that a creative cameraman can give you a degree of nuance and sublety in picture quality that is difficult if not impossible to achieve on videotape. There are certain subjects that almost demand this capability of film. A lovely model in a cosmetic commercial looks lovelier and softer on film. Outdoor scenic beauty is captured better on film. Film can give your commercial a surreal quality, if that's what you want. Film is a more versatile medium than videotape in getting that special look.

The best directors, the best lighting men, the best production houses have traditionally worked in the film medium. However, this is less true now than it was a few years ago. And today most film people will also shoot tape, if you request it. Still, even today, the star directors and the creative production houses prefer the film medium and work best in it. This in itself may cause you to choose film.

Low cost has always been touted as a major advantage in shooting on videotape. However, if you are shooting with a prominent director at a major production house, there is little difference in cost between film and videotape production. On the other hand, if you are shooting a local commercial, and your production budget is small, videotape is much less expensive than film.

Videotaping is faster. There are no film labs involved. But shooting on film and finishing on tape is almost as fast.

When you shoot tape, you see on a monitor exactly what is being recorded. You can immediately play back the scene you've just shot and know whether or not it is what you want. This was one of tape's strong points until recently. Now, however, a tape monitor can be rigged with a film camera so that you see on the monitor what the camera is seeing. And you can play it back after each take.

Tape's three primary advantages of a few years ago—speed, low cost, and seeing what you're getting—are no longer important determining factors in making the film-versus-tape decision. If it's a low-budget local spot, tape is still the answer. If not, you will probably choose between film and tape on the basis of who you want to work with and the kind of "look" you want your commercial to have.

Film Color & Size

Your commercial structure and content will determine whether you shoot in a studio or on location and whether you use film or tape. It will also influence your producer and director in their choice of film size and color. Almost no commercials are filmed in black and white today; color is king. The reasoning is simple: color TV set owners expect to see color. Color production is more expensive than black and white, but the extra dimension of realism it gives a commercial is considered well worth it.

The quality of color film has improved enormously over the years. Tones, shading, and light value can be controlled to a fine degree. Experimentation has widened the range of effects available and made color film an artistic medium of expression.

By carefully planning each scene, your director will include everything you want inside the safety area, the portion of film frame surrounded by the TV cut-off zone. This zone is the area around the perimeter of the TV receiver that does not show the outer portions of each frame of film. Everything inside its circumference will be seen on a TV receiver. And within this area, of course, your action and titles will be placed. Perhaps you have been made aware of this while viewing some old feature film that had titles stretched across the screen. All these would be seen in a theater, but the letters far left and far right are cut off on your home TV screen.

The narrower, smaller, 16mm frame is becoming more popular with amateur movie makers. It is also used for reports on many TV news programs. Sixteen millimeter film is easier to work with than 35mm, and the cameras for 16mm are lighter and more mobile. The film can be less expensive to develop and to edit. But it has some restrictions. Fewer special effects are possible. You have less control over grain, color quality, and tonal values. When 16mm is transferred to videotape or blown up to 35mm, it loses an appreciable percentage of pictorial clarity and intensity; it becomes less sharp.

However, 16mm is ideal for some commercials. Today, some spots are filmed in 16mm to achieve a reportorial, or *cinéma-verité* quality. Handheld cameras move, bounce, pan quickly, zoom in and out. Directors use this technique to gain and transmit a feeling of actuality, of realism and spontaneity. It can be extremely effective, all other facets of the commercial being equal.

Casting

Let us assume that you have created a commercial. The storyboard has been approved and the budget has been signed. How do you and your producer make sure that your commercial will have spontaneity and vitality before you go to the studio to film it? By selecting your actors and announcer with care.

Announcers should be chosen for their voice qualities and the expressive way they read the copy. Actors should be chosen because they best express the characters in the commercial, not because they are fashion-model pretty or handsome. An actor's projection of character, his presence, is the quality to look for. Commercials must involve the viewer emotionally in order to create conviction—and sales. An actor must have conviction himself and express it in a spontaneous manner.

If you work in a small advertising agency, you and your producer will probably do the casting. Large agencies have casting directors on their staffs, usually persons with theatrical experience and entertainment world contacts.

It is absolutely essential that the casting director know precisely the mood and tone of your commercial as well as its objective. Explain your thoughts about the commercial as you discuss the storyboard. Your casting director will have files on all available actors and announcers, with pictures and lists of credits (plays, movies, and commercials that each actor has done). You'll save time by going through the pictures the casting director selects before audition time. But be careful: Some of the pictures may have been taken and retouched years ago.

Auditions

The casting director will then call the actor through his agent and schedule a time spot for an audition. Time can be saved by scheduling actors to appear in ten-minute intervals at the audition room (a large one in your office or at the production house). Fifteen minutes is a more comfortable time allotment for announcers. This will give them the opportunity to go over the script by themselves in the outer waiting room. Also, make sure they have time during the audition to change or alter their reading to gain the special emphasis you want.

You should have a list of the people who will audition, with enough space on the page to write your comments about their audition performance.

When the talent appears and introductions are made, try to put the actor at ease. Even long-time professionals sometimes become nervous at auditions. After a general comment or two, describe the product you are advertising, the commercial, and the specific character you want him to audition for. Give him a few moments to go over the storyboard or script. Then let him read his part aloud, perhaps twice if he's on the right note. Give him suggestions, but do not correct him with a reading of your own. Remember, you are hiring a professional who, with direction at rehearsal and on the set, will give his best characterization. Chances are, he'll give a reading with nuances that you did not know were in the script.

If your commercial has two or more actors with dialogue, audition them together so that you can note stature, mannerisms, and interactions. Write your comments before the next actor or group of actors come into the room to audition. They will be a helpful jog to your memory in later discussions.

Don't waste time—yours or the actor's. Two or three readings should be enough to indicate an actor's proficiency and suitability. And contrary to some Broadway producers' opinions, actors are human beings. Be courteous. Friendly, but professional. This will help build a good attitude on the set when you film your spot.

Some agencies have videotape systems. These can be valuable to you when you cast a commercial. A taped audition is by no means a finished, polished example of an actor's or announcer's work, but it will give you an on-the-spot indication of how well he will perform in your commercial. It will do two more things: Taping can facilitate postaudition reviews with the producer and possibly the client, and the reel of tape can be placed in the agency's archives as part of a growing record of a pool of talent for reference in future casting sessions.

Perhaps your commercial is a testimonial that in-volves actual housewives, mechanics, etc., rather than professional actors. Where do you find them? The fast and easy way is to keep a "lookout" at your product's point of purchase. Make note of each customer. A short interview with selected ones should tell you if you have a potential user-spokesperson for your product. Plan to invite your two top choices to the studio—just in case one "freezes" once the camera is turned on.

Talent Payment

Paying for the talent is the responsibility of the agency casting director and/or producer, but as a creator of commercials, you should know the varying scales. Talent payment and repayment (residuals) can add up to a large part of any commercial's budget. Obviously, 20 men and women, all on camera, all with lines, will be far more costly than two characters who have no lines. It is part of your job to know your talent costs before you go over budget at the storyboard stage.

The Screen Actors Guild (SAG) represents actors who appear in filmed or taped commercials. The American Federation of Television and Radio Artists (AFTRA) is another union to which commercial performers belong. Definite rates or scales of pay have been set for differing appearances in commercials. Actors appearing in spots shown on coast-to-coast networks receive more money than, say, an actor in a commercial shown only in a small local area. An actor who appears as a principal character in a spot receives more pay than another actor in the same spot who appears only as an "extra."

It is not necessary to give all the details about different pay scales here. Let us rather sum up with this guideline: In these cost-conscious times, it is an economic necessity to keep the number of actors in your commercials within the limits of the budget.

Public Service Advertising 13

At a joint meeting of the American Association of Advertising Agencies and the Association of National Advertisers held at Hot Springs, Virginia, in 1941, James Webb Young—then at the J. Walter Thompson agency, but also a professor at the University of Chicago, a farmer in New Mexico, and a philosopher always—delivered a landmark speech in which he said: "Advertising is the most modern, streamlined, high speed means of communication plus persuasion yet invented by man. Because it is this, it has potentialities far beyond its present levels. It ought to be used extensively by governments, by political parties, by labor unions, by farm organizations, by the National Association of Manufacturers, by the great philanthropic foundations, by churches, and by universities. It ought to be used . . . in international relations, to create understanding and reduce friction. It ought to be used to wipe out such diseases of ignorance as childbed fever. It ought to do the nutritional job this country needs to have done. It ought to be the servant of music, of art, of literature and of all the forces of righteousness even more than it is."

The elevation of advertising to this new level of usefulness and public purpose as espoused by Mr. Young in 1941 has continued to this day under the aegis of The Advertising Council, headquartered in New York City, which operates wholly on a voluntary basis. The Advertising Council is a private, nonprofit organization consisting of advertising, business, and media people who have contributed billions of dollars in creative time and advertising to promote improvement in such areas as better health, traffic safety, equal employment opportunity, forest fire prevention, and other vital concerns that affect the general public. Public service advertising is designed to move ideas instead of products, to get something done that needs to be done, and to support human needs and aspirations.

The products of the Council cover four broad areas: (1) developing human resources, (2) promoting citizen awareness, (3) preserving natural resources, and (4) strengthening the economy. The following list, showing the wide and diverse range of public service causes that can be promoted through broadcast commercials of this nature, indicates some of the many areas in which the Advertising Council has served as the coordinator of promotional efforts:

- Aid to higher education
- Peace Corps
- Energy conservation
- Alcoholism: A Treatable Disease
- Child abuse prevention
- American Red Cross
- Religion in American life
- United Negro College Fund
- National Organization on Disability
- High blood pressure education
- United States Savings Bonds
- International Youth Exchange

On occasion, manufacturers conduct public service campaigns on their own. For example, Shell Oil Co. sponsored a series of "Bicentennial Minutes" in 1976 in an effort to educate American television viewers about the events that led up to the founding of the United States.

Public service commercials on radio and television can and do use most of the formats discussed in Chapter 3. No matter which format they employ, however, the appeal is frequently to the emotions. It is difficult to be unemotional about deaths caused by air pollution, pain and suffering that results from ignorance, or injuries to children caused by rodents in run-down big-city tenements.

The radio and television spots on the following pages are outstanding examples of public service advertising.

Exhibit 13-1. Public Service: American Cancer Society

Advertiser: American Cancer Society   Title: ''Yes You Can''

Agency: Bentley, Barnes & Lynn, Inc.   Format: Spokesman

Service: Cancer prevention   Length: 30 seconds

MAN: If you're gonna get it, you're gonna get it.

ANNCR: Not so. You <u>can</u> prevent cancer. 60% of cancer can be prevented.

WOMAN: My sister had it. So what can I do?

ANNCR: You <u>can</u> do something. The American Cancer Society has a new brochure, "Yes You Can." It explains how you can <u>prevent</u> cancer...<u>detect</u> cancer... <u>beat</u> cancer. For your free copy, call 800-572-1021.

MAN: I mean, everything causes cancer, right?

ANNCR: Wrong.

Exhibit 13-2. Public Service: Mormon Church

Advertiser: Mormon Church

Agency: Bonneville Productions

Service: Moral advice

Title: "It Isn't Fair"

Format: Testimonial

Length: 60 seconds

ANNCR: It isn't fair.

WOMAN: You're ugly. You're fat. And that's what I think in bed at night and I hate myself. That's when I'm loneliest. And being single I really want to belong to someone. Sometimes I just whisper I love you when there's no one there to say it to. Sometimes I just pretend there's someone else saying that to me too.

ANNCR: It just isn't fair.

WOMAN: But being lonely doesn't make me bad. Being lonely doesn't mean I have to hate myself. I'm learning to like myself more and more all the time, and I like me. I really do. But maybe that's why I feel lonely. Because I am important.

ANNCR: It isn't fair. It's life. And sometimes it hurts. But it's not what life does to you. It's what you do with life. From the Mormons, The Church of Jesus Christ of Latter-day Saints.

Exhibit 13-3. Public Service: United Negro College Fund

Advertiser: United Negro College Fund

Agency: Ad Council/Young & Rubicam

Service: Support of black education

Title: "Myrtilla Miller"

Formats: Slice of life/Spokesman

Length: 60 seconds

SFX:_ _ _ _ _ _ _ _ _	CRACKLING_OF_FIRE_
VOICES:	Get some more wood over here. All right. Here, gimme the torch.
SFX:_ _ _ _ _ _ _ _ _	CRACKLING_BECOMES_A_BLAZE.
VOICES:	There it goes. We'll teach her. You'd think a white woman'd know better.
ANNCR:	In 1860, Myrtilla Miner, a white woman, had started a school for black children in Rhode Island. She was harassed in the daily press and forced to move from place to place. Miss Miner did everything possible to keep her school open ... until it was burned down. To commemorate her ideals and courage, a college in Washington, D.C., was named in her honor: The Miner Teachers College. Supporting black education once meant putting your life or liberty on the line. Fortunately, today we just need your signature. Please write a check to the United Negro College Fund. And continue a great American tradition. A mind is a terrible thing to waste.
ANNCR. #2:	A public service message of this station and The Advertising Council.

Exhibit 13-4. Public Service: The American Red Cross

Advertiser: The American Red Cross

Agency: Ad Council/J. Walter Thompson Co.

Service: Emergency medical aid

Title: "The Train"

Format: Narrative

Length: 30 seconds

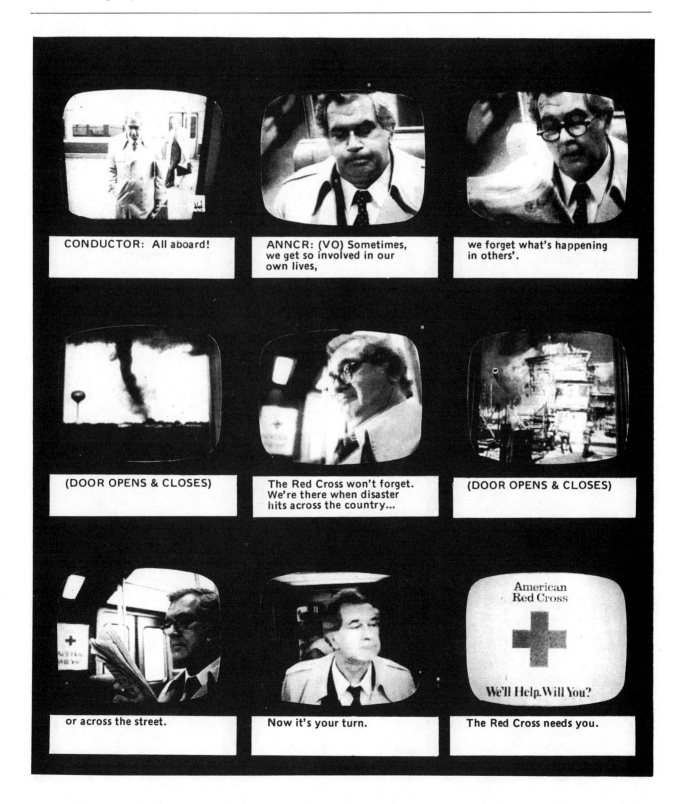

Exhibit 13-5. Public Service: Alliance to Save Energy

Advertiser: Alliance to Save Energy

Agency: Ad Council/J. Walter Thompson Co.

Service: Energy conservation

Title: ''Slithering Energy''

Formats: Slice of life/Spokesman

Length: 60 seconds

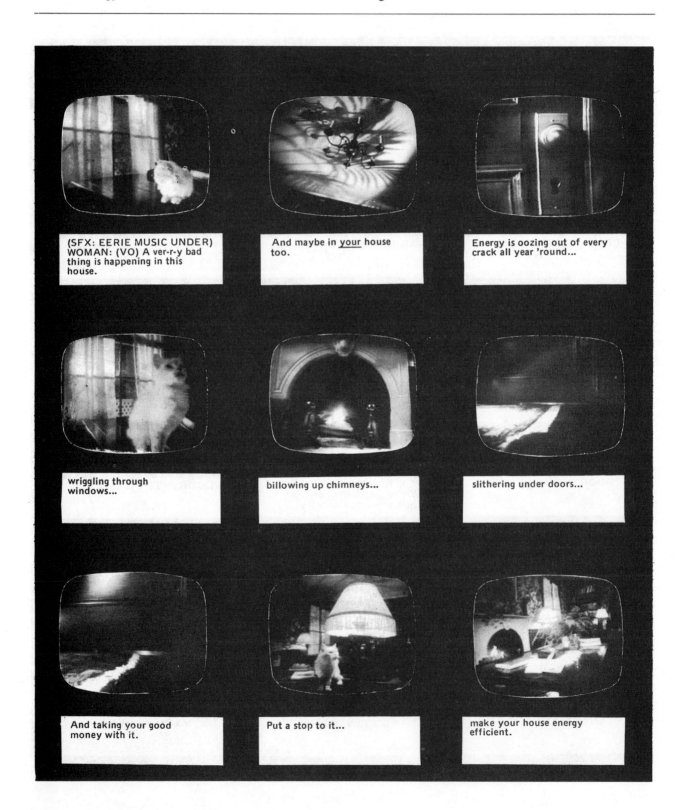

(SFX: EERIE MUSIC UNDER) WOMAN: (VO) A ver-r-y bad thing is happening in this house.

And maybe in your house too.

Energy is oozing out of every crack all year 'round...

wriggling through windows...

billowing up chimneys...

slithering under doors...

And taking your good money with it.

Put a stop to it...

make your house energy efficient.

Seal up all the leaks... insulate and install energy-saving appliances.

WOMAN: (OC) Put a stop to it. A house that saves energy

is worth more and costs less to run.

An energy efficient house may get you a better mortgage...or a bigger bank loan.

So, save energy...and keep your money where... your house is.

Federal Home Loan
Mortgage Corporation

Federal National
Mortgage Association

National Institute
of Building Sciences

WOMAN: (VO) A message from these organizations and

ALLIANCE TO SAVE ENERGY
BOX 57200
WASHINGTON, D.C. 20037

A Public Service of This Slot on & The Advertising Council

the Alliance to Save Energy. For more information, write the Alliance.

Exhibit 13-6. Public Service: The Crime Prevention Coalition

Advertiser: The Crime Prevention Coalition

Agency: Ad Council/Dancer Fitzgerald Sample, Inc.

Service: Crime prevention

Title: ''Jenny''

Format: Spokesman

Length: 60 seconds

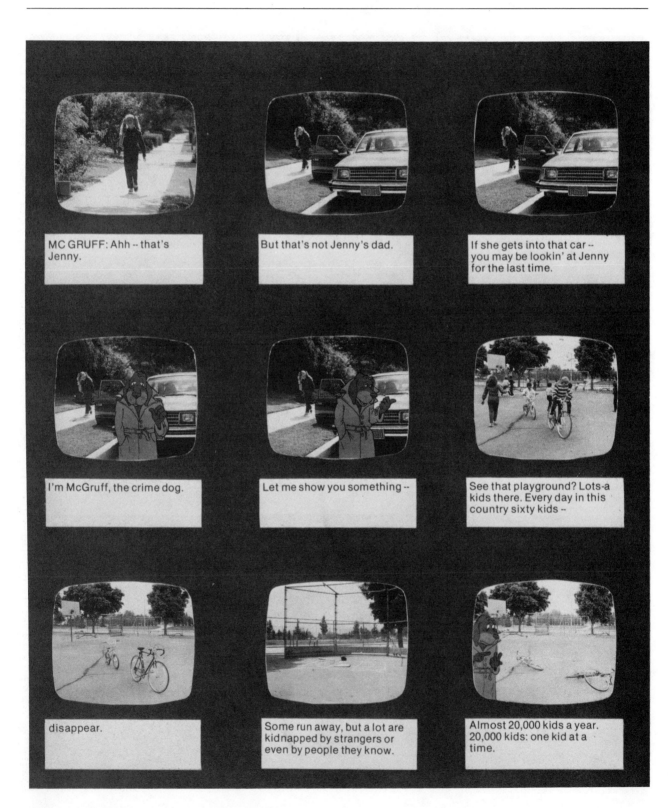

MC GRUFF: Ahh -- that's Jenny.

But that's not Jenny's dad.

If she gets into that car -- you may be lookin' at Jenny for the last time.

I'm McGruff, the crime dog.

Let me show you something --

See that playground? Lots-a kids there. Every day in this country sixty kids --

disappear.

Some run away, but a lot are kidnapped by strangers or even by people they know.

Almost 20,000 kids a year. 20,000 kids: one kid at a time.

Maybe your kid. On your street.

Just like Jenny.

You know, your kids can learn to protect themselves against crime -- at home, at school, on the street.

Very nice going, Jenny.

She's gonna tell her folks about this.

And you can write to McGruff. Learn how to keep your family and your community safe.

And help take a bite out of crime.
(RUFF)

Glossaries 14

Radio

Account A sponsor who has entered into a contract with a station or network; also a contract between a sponsor and an advertising agency or representative.

Across the board A program presented five days a week at the same time each day.

Ad-lib To announce or talk without a prepared script.

AFTRA American Federation of Television and Radio Artists. A national labor organization representing people in radio and television, especially performers (talent).

Aircheck A recording of a program or commercial.

Airman Also called announcer or personality. Someone who is performing on the air (e.g., a disc jockey).

Airshift Or ''show'' time when talent is on the air.

Allocation The specific assignment of frequency and power to a station by the Federal Communications Commission.

Audition The testing, usually in a studio, of talent for a particular role in a commercial or a specific job for a performance.

Back-timing Timing the last two or three stories of a newscast, speech, or music, etc., in a program to enable the talent to get off the air on time.

Block programing The scheduling of programs of similar appeal back-to-back to keep listeners from switching to another station.

Board The control panel through which the broadcast program passes.

Bulletin The first brief announcement of an important news event.

Call letters Letters assigned to a station by the FCC.

Cart A cassette-type cartridge. Used for taped announcements, jingles, commercials, music, or bridges, etc.

Call letters Letters assigned to a station by the FCC.

Clearing music Obtaining releases (approval) from the copyright holders of music, or ascertaining whether the station, as a result of contracts with organizations holding copyrights (ASCAP, BMI) is privileged to present a musical selection.

Close The closing announcement to a program.

Cluster buster A line or phrase to break up back-to-back commercial announcements.

Commentary A selection of a program devoted to opinion.

Commercial Advertising; sometimes called a ''spot.''

Continuity writer One who creates radio copy other than news.

Cough button A small switch attached to mike or on studio control panel which, when pressed, cuts mike off while talent clears his throat.

Cue A signal, either verbal or by sign. Also, ''cue a record,'' the act of preparing a record to be played on the air without an opening ''wow.''

Cut a record To make a recording or transcription; also, ''make a tape'' or ''lay down a tape.''

Dateline program A news program written in bulletin style with each story beginning with the name of the city or location in which the story originated.

Dead air Unintentional silence on the air.

DGA Directors Guild of America. A national organization representing film, television, and radio directors.

Drive time Those morning and late-afternoon hours when commuters are driving to and from work.

Dub or dubbing Transferring material from one record or tape to another.

Fade A decrease in volume.

Fading in Increasing volume so that music, sound, or speech rises in volume gradually.

Feedback The return of sound from a loudspeaker to the mike in which it originated; also, public response to station management either in complaint or praise.

Feeding The delivery of a program over a telephone hookup either to a network or some other point.

Fluff A mistake in delivery by talent.

Format The type of programing a station uses (e.g., classical, all news, top forty, MOR, beautiful music).

Frequency discount A discount given by a network or

station to a sponsor who buys commercial time in large quantities.

Fuzzy Applies to program or line that is not clear.

Gain Control of volume; usually called "riding gain."

Guideline A one-word description of a news story. Also called "slug" or "slugline."

I.D. Station call letters followed by location (e.g., WBCB . . . Levittown-Fairless Hills).

Independent station A local, commercial station not affiliated with any network, usually found in the larger markets.

Jingle A musical commercial for product, service, or station.

Jumping cue When an announcer or newscaster starts a program before he is scheduled to begin.

Level The volume noted on the meter (potentiometer) of the control board. A knob sometimes called a "pot."

Line A telephone line (wire) used for the transmission of a program.

Live announcement A message read in person, not prerecorded.

Live mike A microphone that is turned on.

Log A record or schedule of everything broadcast; required by the FCC.

Monitoring Listening to a program.

MOR A format used by many stations featuring middle-of-the-road-type music.

NAB National Association of Broadcasters. A trade organization devoted to promoting radio and TV stations.

NABET National Association of Broadcast Engineers and Technicians. A labor organization.

Nemo A program originating outside of the local studio.

News analyst One who reports, analyzes, and comments on news.

Newscaster One who reads straight news on the air and who may or may not write his own news for on-air delivery.

News editor One who rewrites, edits, and supervises the news program. May also deliver news on the air.

O & O stations Broadcasting stations "owned and operated" by a network. Usually very successful stations in large markets that contribute handsomely to a network's total profit.

Open An introductory announcement to a program.

Optional copy Additional news items that announcer or newscaster can use if he runs short of copy.

Overmodulating Putting too much volume over the air; sometimes called "blasting."

Participating sponsor A client who shares commercial time with other sponsors of the same program.

PBS Public Broadcasting System. A nonprofit radio and TV network.

Printer A teletype machine.

Protection An extra take, to be used in case the selected take is ruined or lost.

PSA A public service announcement.

Public domain (or PD) Program or commercial content not protected by copyright that may be used freely without payment of a fee. PD can also mean program director.

RAB Radio Advertising Bureau.

Ratings Statistical measurements of a station's audience.

Reading cold Reading a program or a news story on the air without having rehearsed it.

Release Copy sent in advance to be held for use at a designated time.

Remote A program picked up from outside the studio (e.g., football games, reports from the scene of a fire or flood).

Rewrite A news story or program that undergoes revision.

RTNDA Radio-Television News Directors Association.

Special event On-the-scene broadcast of a news event, usually planned.

Spot A commercial, either recorded or delivered live.

Standby A program used in emergencies.

Stand by A cue to performers before they are given a live microphone.

Station break Or just "break." A pause to permit local stations to identify themselves.

Sustainer A program that is not sponsored.

Tack-up A news program prepared by pasting or stapling wire copy to sheets of copy paper and then editing the stories.

Take A performance attempt. When recording, each attempt is given a number: "Take One," "Take Two," etc. The take deemed most satisfactory is then used.

Talk-over When an airman talks during the first few bars of a musical selection.

Ticket A license granted by the FCC.

Time copy Copy for news or a live commercial that is back-timed.

Traffic A station or network department that receives orders for commercials, makes certain that they get on the air, and then follows up in billing advertisers.

Triple-spotting Running three separate commercials in one commercial time period.

Wire copy News, sports, weather, and information printed by a teletype machine, usually originating from the Associated Press, United Press International, or another news service.

Woof The sound made by an engineer into a microphone to synchronize audio levels.

WX A symbol for weather.

Television

AAAA American Association of Advertising Agencies, or the 4 A's. A national organization of advertising agencies devoted to standardizing procedures and upgrading the business level of its members.

Above the line Motion picture, television, or radio costs relating to artistic or creative elements in production (writing, acting, directing, music, etc.). (Compare with **Below the line.**)

Abstract set A nonrepresentational setting using elements such as drapes, columns, steps, platforms, free-standing flats with various textures and geometrical forms, etc. Such a setting has no definite locale, but may suggest one.

Academy field When you look through the lens of a motion picture camera, you see two sets of lines framing the rectangular scene. The larger represents what will be seen when the film is projected on a regular screen; this is "academy field" or "academy framing." The smaller set of lines defines the TV field (or "TV cutoff") and shows what will appear on the TV screen. In filming a TV commercial, all essential elements in a scene should be confined to the smaller area.

Academy leader On a TV commercial print or other film print, the section of film with a series of "countdown" numbers to enable the projectionist to cue the opening scene or title of the picture.

Across the board A show that airs at the same time five days a week. So called because it appears straight across the program board each of the first five days.

Action Any movement that takes place in front of a camera or on film. Any movement that carries the story forward and develops the plot.

A.D. Abbreviation for assistant director; a member of the production crew who handles details relating to the actual shooting of a commercial, such as cast and crew calls, adherence to production schedules, etc.

Adjacencies Commercials or programs that immediately precede or follow one another.

Ad-lib To extemporize lines or music not written into the script or the musical score.

Advertising Council The joint body of the AAAA and the ANA (Association of National Advertisers) and media, through which public service projects are developed and channeled to advertisers for their support (e.g., Smokey the Bear, Cancer Crusade, etc.).

Affiliate A television or radio station associated by contract with a network.

AFTRA Abbreviation for American Federation of Television and Radio Artists, a member of AFL, made up of actors, singers, announcers, etc. It is concerned only with commercials made on videotape or televised live; regulates wage scales for its members.

Screen Actors Guild (SAG) serves the same function for talent appearing in filmed commercials. Many performers belong to both unions.

Aided recall A research interviewing technique in which the respondent is given a hint or reminder to elicit a meaningful response. The opposite of this is a "free response" in which the person being interviewed is not given a hint.

Aircheck A recording, either audio or video, or both, of an actual broadcast. It serves as a file copy of a program or commercial for an agency, a sponsor, or a competitive sponsor.

Alternate sponsorship When two advertisers share a single program with one advertiser dominant one week and the other the following week (or whenever the programs are scheduled).

Angle of view The amount of horizontal area of a scene that registers on a lens. Varies in proportion to size of lens, from narrow to wide angle.

Angle shot A camera shot taken from any position except straight on the subject.

Animation Creating an illusion of motion by photographing a series of drawings so that we see drawings that move. Usually done in a cartoon style. Sometimes combined with live action on film.

Announcement spot A brief commercial not integrated into the program.

Announcer (1) The member of a radio or television station staff assigned the duty of introducing and describing program features; (2) the station staff member who delivers a commercial live; (3) the talent who delivers the commercial message (or part of it) either on camera or as a voice-over.

Answer print The first "completed" print of a commercial for client approval. It contains picture, voice track, music, opticals, etc. Color correction and sound levels may be changed before the commercial is telecast.

Arc A strong, blue-white light that glows as a result of electricity sparking across two carbon electrodes (as opposed to a filament that glows from heat).

Arri Nickname for an Arriflex camera, 35mm, widely used in making filmed commercials.

ASCAP American Society of Composers, Authors and Publishers; a music-licensing organization.

Audience accumulation An increase in audience achieved by broadcasting a program in a series rather than just once.

Audience composition A term that refers to a classification of the individuals or the households in a television or radio audience into various categories. Common categories for individuals are age and sex groupings (e.g., men, women, teenagers, and children). Common categories for households are based on the number of members of the household, age or education of the head of the household, household income, and so forth.

Audience flow The statistical composition of the total audience of a program showing the parts (1) retained from the previous program, (2) transferred from another station, and (3) tuned in for the first time.

Audience profile A demographic description of the people exposed to a program or commercial.

Audience share The number or proportion of all home sets in use that are tuned to a particular program.

Audimeter An electronic rating research device. This device is used by the A. C. Nielsen Co. to record the radio and TV tuning of sets in selected homes.

Audio The sound portion of a TV broadcast.

Audition A tryout of actors, announcers, musicians, or programs.

Availability In broadcasting, a time period available for purchase by an agency for an advertiser. For talent, the word is used to refer to the artist's lack of conflict either in a product category or for a recording or shooting date.

Average audience rating A type of rating computed for some specified interval of time, such as for the length of a television or radio program or for a 15- or 30-minute period.

Background A broadcasting sound effect, musical or otherwise, used behind or under the dialogue or other program elements. In TV storyboards, the letters ''BG'' refer to the setting behind the actors, figures, or products in the foreground.

Back light Illumination from behind the subject and opposite the camera.

Back to back A broadcast situation in which two or more commercials directly follow each other without a break. (Also called ''piggyback.'')

Balop Generally, any opaque projector or the slides and art work prepared for it. The projector consists of (1) an illuminated stage or surface to hold the object to be televised and (2) a lens placed to project the image on the tube in the pickup camera. Multistage balops permit dissolves, superimpositions, and simple animation.

Balopticon (balops) A type of television animation made possible through the use of a Balopticon machine, usually in a TV station.

Basic network The section of a national television or radio network covering the more populous markets.

BCU (TCU, ECU) An extremely narrow angle picture. Big close-up. Tight close-up. Extreme close-up.

Below the line Motion picture, television, or radio costs relating to the technical or material elements in production (props, sets, equipment, staging services, etc.).

Billboard An announcement at the beginning of a broadcast that lists the sponsor and/or products featured in the program.

Bit A small part in a television program or commercial.

Bridge Music or sound effect linking two scenes in a TV or radio program.

Business An actor's movement, especially with props; action used to add interest to a program or commercial.

Busy Describes a setting or background that is too elaborate, thereby diverting the viewer's attention from the actors or object that should predominate.

Buy-out Compensation for a performer not according to the prevailing scale with residual benefits, but in one complete and final sum.

Call letters Initials assigned by the Federal Communications Commission to identify a station.

Camera rehearsal Similar to a dress rehearsal in stage vernacular, in which all talent is present and in costume and the complete production is shot by cameramen for final check before telecasting.

Channel A band of radio frequencies assigned to a given radio or TV station, or assigned to other broadcasting purposes.

Circulation The number of households or individuals, regardless of where located, that are estimated to be in the audience of a given television or radio network or station at least once during some specified period of time (e.g., one week or one month). Thus, circulation is simply a term used to describe the size of the cumulative audience of a network or a station over some period of time.

Class (A, B, C) rates The charges or fees for different time segments on a TV or radio station. The most desirable and costly TV time is usually between 6:00 and 11:00 PM. Rates vary from city to city and from station to station.

Clear (1) To obtain legal permission from responsible sources to use a musical selection, photograph, film clip, or quotation for use in an advertisement. (2) To arrange for approval from a station for a certain time slot for a program or commercial.

Close-up A shot of an individual with the camera moved in close so that only the head and shoulders fill the screen. A big close-up (BCU) may include only the head or perhaps just the eyes. A close-up shot (CU) may also be taken of an object.

Closed circuit A television program that is distributed to specific television receivers but not telecast to the public.

Coincidental A method of checking the viewers of a program by phoning a sample of possible viewers while the program is in progress.

Commercial The advertiser's message on television or radio.

Continuity (1) Script for a television or radio program. (2) The flow or sequential development of a commercial.

Control room The room adjacent to the television studio or recording studio, from which the video and/or audio is coordinated.

Cost per thousand The ratio of the cost of a television or radio advertisement (in dollars) to a number of households (in thousands) or to a number of individuals (in thousands) estimated to be in the audience at the time the advertisement is broadcast. The term is more fully referred to as "cost per thousand households (or homes)" or "cost per thousand viewers."

Coverage Conceptually, the number of households or individuals, regardless of where located, that are able to receive a given television or radio station or group of stations.

Cowcatcher An isolated commercial announcement at the beginning of a program that advertises a "secondary" product of the sponsor. This secondary product is not mentioned in the program itself.

Crab dolly Generally, a camera move in which the camera pans the subject while the dolly (the camera's moveable base) is being moved.

Crawl Graphics (usually credit copy) that move slowly up the screen; usually mounted on a drum that can also be called a "crawl."

Cross-fade In television, the fading out of one picture and the simultaneous fading in of another. In radio, the fading out of dialogue, sound, or music, while simultaneously fading in other dialogue, sound, or music.

CU A close-up shot. Narrow angle picture. Usually bust or head shot of person or full-screen image of object.

Cue (1) The final words of an announcer's speech or actor's line used as a signal for another actor or announcer to begin. (2) A sound or musical effect. (3) A manual or audio signal from a director calling for action.

Cut (1) A signal to stop performers. (2) The deletion of program material to fit a prescribed period of time. (3) The simplest transition from one TV commercial scene to another—in which the final frame of one scene changes abruptly to that of another scene.

Cut-in The insertion of a local announcement on cue into a network or transcribed program. Also termed a "cut-in announcement" or a "local cut-in."

Cut to (1) A fast switch from the picture on one camera to the picture on another. (2) An abrupt change of scene without a dissolve or wipe.

Demographic characteristics As used in broadcast research, a broad term that refers to the various social and economic characteristics of a group of households, or a group of individuals. For example, the term is used to refer to such characteristics as the number of members of a household, age of head of household, occupation of head of household, education of household members, and annual household income.

Depth of field The distance within which a subject can move toward or away from the camera without going out of focus, assuming no camera adjustment.

Diary method A panel method designed to study broadcast audiences for short periods of time, usually one week.

Diorama A miniature setting, complete in detail and perspective, used as a means of establishing large locations impossible to construct or restage in the studio.

Director (1) In TV and radio programing, the person responsible for the rehearsal and performance. (2) For commercials, the person who rehearses actors and announcers, guides cameramen, orders lighting effects, and works with the producer—in short, the person in charge on the set or location.

Dissolve (DS or DISS) (1) A combination fade-in and fade-out; a new scene appears while the preceding scene vanishes. When an object in the first scene apparently remains on screen for the second scene, it is called a "match dissolve." (2) Transitional device to indicate lapse of time by shifting the camera image slowly from one picture to another. (3) The overlapping fade-out of one picture and fade-in of another.

Dolly A moveable carriage usually mounted on four wheels that carries either a camera or a camera and cameraman.

Dolly camera A TV camera mounted on a small boom that is mounted on a four-wheel base. Has the advantage of greater height and mobility. It requires a special dolly pusher.

Dolly in To move in from a distance for a close-up by means of a camera mounted on a dolly.

Dolly out The reverse of dolly in. (Dolly back.)

Down and under A direction denoting that voices, music, and sound effects should now be heard at a lower level.

Drop-in In broadcasting, a local commercial inserted in a nationally sponsored network program.

Dry runs Those rehearsals previous to camera rehearsals in which business, lines, sets, etc. are perfected.

Dubbing (1) Recording actor's and/or announcer's lip sync to film already shot. (2) A copying of an audio tape.

ECU Abbreviation for extreme close-up. A shot showing only a portion of a face or other object. (See also: **BCU, TCU**.)

Establishing shot A view of a scene wide and deep enough to establish the relationships of the people and objects in it.

E.T. An electrical transcription. Similar to a record except that it is produced solely for radio and television stations.

Extra A person, usually one of many, used in background shots, crowd shots, parties, etc. Such persons generally have no lines or dialogue.

Fade-in To gradually increase the intensity of a video picture from black to full scene.

Fade-out From full brightness, a picture gradually disappears until the screen is dark. The decreasing of signal strength.

Fixed focus The focus of the lens is not changed regardless of what movement takes place in front of the camera.

Flash cut To intersperse scenes of a second or less.

Flat Lack of contrast in a screen image. Also, term for a scenic unit.

Floor manager The production man who heads the crew in a live television studio. Transmits the control director's instructions to actors and others on set.

"Follow" shot The camera follows the movement of the subject without necessarily moving itself.

Frame In motion pictures, a single picture of the many that make up the whole. In television, the field of view in any particular shot. Adjustments in this are known as framing. An improper adjustment is off frame. When the subject crowds the sides of the picture, it is tight framing; when there is plenty of room, it is loose framing.

Free-lance A self-employed person who works independently, not employed by an agency or company.

Freeze frame A film technique of holding a particular frame still on the screen for a desired length. Often used at the close of a commercial.

Fringe time In television, the hours before or after prime viewing hours.

From the top An order to start rehearsal from the very beginning of the musical number or script. May also refer to the start of a scene currently being rehearsed.

Full shot A full-length view of actors or talent.

Go to black The picture is gradually faded out; same as fade to black, fade-out.

Golden time Whenever filming of a TV commercial runs overtime, the costs mount rapidly; this time is considered to be "golden."

Grip The general handyman available on the set for such odd jobs as moving or adjusting sets or repairing props.

Hand-hold To make a shot with the camera held in the hands. Also, a handle that can be mounted on a camera for this purpose.

Head shot A close-up of an actor's or announcer's head, usually from the shoulders up.

Hiatus A break in the advertiser's broadcast schedule.

Hitchhike A short commercial tagged on the end of a program, advertising another product of the company sponsoring the program. When at the front, it is a "cowcatcher."

I.D. Station identification; a 10-second spot on television used at station breaks. Time enough for the product name and claim—and a lot of creative ingenuity.

Integrated commercial A multiple-product TV commercial in which two or more products are presented within the framework of a single announcement.

Interlock Any arrangement permitting the synchronous presentation of picture and matching sound from separate films. The simplest consists of a mechanical link connecting projector and sound reproducer, both being driven by a common synchronous drive.

Key lighting Pinpoint, intense light focused on a small area for highlight effect.

Kinescope The tube currently used in receivers or monitors on which the TV picture is reproduced. Trade name developed by RCA.

Kinescope film A television program filmed directly from a kinescope tube.

Kinescope recording A reproduction on film of a TV program or commercial taken directly from the face or screen of the kinescope receiver tube.

Lap dissolve Cross fading of one scene or image over another. Momentarily both pictures are visible. One picture disappears as another picture appears.

Leader (academy leader) The film that precedes the commercial opening. Usually 10 seconds. It has positioning and focus references to guide the video engineer, and numbers sequenced in seconds from nine down to three. Then the film is black for three seconds before the opening frame of the commercial.

"Limbo" shot Pictures taken against nonrecognized background. Often used with close-ups where background is nonessential.

Level The amount or quantity of loudness of sound. Also, level of light.

Lip-synchronization (lip-sync) Recording of a voice or voices to match the exact movement of actors' lips in a film already recorded. Or it can mean the filming of scenes with actors' lips moving to match a prerecorded track.

Live In television, a program or commercial that is being telecast as it originates.

Location The place or area away from a film studio in which a commercial or other part might be filmed.

Logotype (logo) The sponsor's or brand name's identifying signature or trademark.

LS Long shot. A full view of a set or background usually including a full-length view of actor or actors.

Make-good Credit for a missed commercial or program or rebroadcast in a comparable time period to make up for one unavoidably cancelled, omitted, or not shown clearly or in its entirety.

Matting (matte) A technique in which one part of a picture is photographed in one location and another in a different location, and then the two are combined in the printing process so that they appear to have been photographed at the same time and place.

Medium shot Somewhere between a close-up and a long shot.

Mix The sound studio session at which two or three or more sound tracks are combined.

Mobile unit Field equipment housed in special trucks for the televising or taping of an event remote from the studio.

Monitor A control kinescope used by personnel (producer, switcher, technical director) to check and preview camera pickups or on-the-air pictures.

Montage A sequence of short scenes that together convey an idea that could not be conveyed by any one of them alone. Sometimes several of the scenes appear on the screen at once; sometimes one blends into another; sometimes they appear in quick succession.

Move in A storyboard designation describing camera movement toward the subject being photographed. Also "zoom in."

Moviola A special machine (with sound equipment) used mainly by editors for viewing film in small size.

MS Abbreviation for medium shot. Somewhere between a close-up (CU) and a long shot (LS).

MS and MCU Medium shot and medium close-up. Camera instructions indicating that the subject should be seen in relation to some but not all other elements in a scene, the latter being more restrictive than the former.

Narrator An off-camera or background voice. Refers also to an on-camera spokesman relating the story line of a script.

Network Interconnecting broadcasting stations for the simultaneous broadcasting of TV or radio programs.

NTI Nielsen Television Index. A limited but projectable rating system that helps determine a TV program's viewing audience.

Off-camera An actor or announcer's voice that is heard although the actor or announcer does not appear on screen.

Off-screen narration Any narration that is not lip-sync. Also referred to as "voice-over."

On-camera (1) An actor or announcer delivers his lines as he appears on the screen. (2) Whatever is included within the scope of the lens.

Opaques Nontransparent art work or visuals (i.e., a photo, postcard, picture from a magazine, etc.). Variations: (1) "Flip": opaque art work or titles mounted on a heavy card, flipped vertically or horizontally. (2) Draw cards: some material pulled manually or mechanically from its position, either horizontally, vertically, or obliquely.

Open end (1) A broadcast in which the commercial spots are added locally. (2) A network commercial complete except for the final seconds of audio or video that are cut in locally.

Optical Special photographic effects, such as the dissolving of one scene into another, wiping out of one scene and appearance of another (wipe), a motion picture within the film (matte shot), grouping of several scenes simultaneously (montage), etc.

Optical view finder The device on a camera used by the cameraman to accurately frame and focus the scene to be televised or filmed.

Over scale A rate of pay that is more than the standard rate of pay for a particular job. Star personalities often demand, and receive, over-scale compensation.

Over-the-shoulder shot A camera shot of a performer from across the shoulder of the character to whom he is speaking.

Pan An abbreviation of panoramic. To "pan" is to move the camera, either left or right, without moving the dolly or base. A movement up or down is properly called a "tilt," but on some scripts you will see the direction "pan up" instead of "tilt up."

Participating program A TV or radio show in which a number of advertisers have their products featured or mentioned.

Pedestal camera A TV camera mounted on a pneumatically controlled base allowing for greater movement in the studio. Must be moved by a cameraman or operator.

Picture resolution The clarity with which the TV image appears on the TV screen.

Piggyback A one-minute time segment in which a sponsor can show two commercials, each featuring a different product.

Playback The replaying of a tape for review and correction purposes.

Positive A projection print from negative film. The true picture.

Preempt Telecasting time made available for a special event, which takes the place of the regularly scheduled program.

Primetime A continuous period of not less than three hours of the broadcast day during which the station's audience is the greatest. In television, usually from 7:00 to 11:00 PM in the East and from 6:00 to 10:00 PM in the Midwest and West.

Prism lens A special lens with several facets that breaks one picture up into many. Used for special effects—as when multiple images of a dancer are seen on many parts of the screen.

Process shot A shot involving an unusual process of some sort, especially rear projection (either still or in motion), with live action taking place in front of the projected picture; shooting through glass on which scenes are painted, with live action taking place behind it; or the use of miniature sets combined with live action in such a way as to create the impression of reality.

Producer The coordinator and overseer of all aspects of getting a TV storyboard onto film or tape. Responsible for budget, schedules, talent, and meeting deadlines.

Product protection In television, the assurance to an advertiser of a time lapse between his commercial and that of a competitor. Given by a station or network, such protection assurance is usually up to 15 minutes.

Promo Spot ad plugging a program, station, or service.

Props From "properties." All the articles in a production that are the property of the producing company or are rented by the company; notably furnishings and decorations, but including an infinite variety of items, large and small, from ashtrays to zipguns.

Pull-back A storyboard designation describing camera movement away from the subject being photographed. (Also zoom-back, move-back.)

Rate card A chart that lists the cost of broadcast time on a station based on the length of the announcement and the number of times it is used on the air.

Rating The percentage of a statistical sample of families who have a radio and/or television set available and who reported hearing or viewing a particular program when interviewed.

Rating points In broadcast, the percent of potential audience tuned to a specific station for a specific program.

Rear projection A device that allows actors to be filmed in front of a screen on which is projected—from behind—a special background. A substitute for expensive location shooting. A device that allows an actor or announcer to be on camera while the background can be anything you want.

Release print The final print of a commercial film or kinescope to be delivered to a TV station, client, or agency.

Remote A telecast originated outside the studio.

Reportage The style of shooting film with a hand-held camera, available light, and candidness. Kind of a *cinéma verité* technique that gives the film added realism, an unrehearsed quality.

Run-through A rehearsal.

SAG Screen Actors Guild. The union of performers in films who work for established scales of pay. The only time you may use a player who is not a member of SAG is when you are showing actual jobs or activities that non-SAG people alone are qualified to do.

Saturation A media term denoting high frequency of advertising impressions during a concentrated period of time.

Scale The standard, established rates of pay for members of film and television unions.

Scene A completed piece of action or dialogue. Usually all the action and dialogue taking place continuously with the same background. Also, a setting or location for action.

Segue In music, the bridge or transition from one theme to another.

Set A TV scene used or constructed in the studio in which action takes place and is filmed.

Share of audience Generally, the percentage of the aggregate television or radio audience in some specified area of a given network, station, or program. Frequently referred to simply as "share."

Shock cut Sudden, abrupt cut to a particular dramatic scene or action.

Shooting date The day designated for the start of actual filming.

Signature The name and/or logo or trademark of the advertiser.

Simulcast The simultaneous playing of a program over television and radio. (Also, a stereo broadcast over two radio stations.)

Slide A title or picture on a single frame of 35mm film that is projected into the camera. Called "transparencies," they are invariably glass mounted. (May be other than 35mm in size.)

Sneak To bring in a sound or a music cue at low volume without distracting the attention of the listener. After an effect has served its purpose, it may be "sneaked out" in like manner.

SOF Sound on film.

Sound effects (SFX) Various devices or recordings used to simulate lifelike sounds. On storyboards, use the abbreviation SFX before you indicate the sound effect you wish.

Spec sheet A list of specifications about a product or advertiser, to be included in a commercial by an announcer who creates his own wording for the commercial. (Also, fact sheet.)

Special effects Miniatures, diorama, or various electrical, film, or mechanical devices used to simulate impressive backgrounds, massive titles, etc. Any trick device used to achieve scenic or dramatic effects impossible in actual or full-scale production in the TV studio.

Splice To join together two pieces of film with film cement.

Split screen A special effect utilizing two or more cameras so that two or more scenes are visible simultaneously on separate parts of the screen (e.g., two people holding a telephone conversation).

Sponsor The firm or individual that pays for broadcast time and talent.

Spot (1) Spotlight. (2) Time segment of one minute or less sold by stations for advertisements.

Spot commercial Commercial of one minute or less, usually on film or tape. It may be shown within a program or adjacent to it.

Spot television Generally, commercial messages within shows not totally sponsored by one firm or commercials shown during station breaks, as opposed to commercials within the framework of one sponsor's program. Also, the spotting of commercials in selected geographical locations.

Sound track The recorded audio portion of a filmed or taped commercial.

Station break A brief break in the programing so that a station may identify itself. An "hour" network program actually runs only 59 minutes and 25 seconds, the next five seconds being used for network identification, the following 20 for a commercial, and the final 10 for another commercial including two seconds for local station identification. A half-hour network program runs 29 minutes and 25 seconds.

Still A still photograph or other illustrative material that may be used in a TV broadcast.

Stock shot A scene not filmed especially for the production, but taken from film files or a film library.

Stop motion Film taken by exposing one frame instead of many frames at a time. An object or objects are usually moved a fraction of an inch for each exposure according to a predetermined pattern.

Storyboard Drawings or photographs arranged in sequence that show the visual continuity of a commercial, with copy adjacent to each picture describing the video action and the audio portion.

Studio (1) At a TV station, a room from which programs emanate. (2) At a film production house, the room in which commercials are filmed.

Super Abbreviation for superimposition. One picture (usually opaque titles) is imposed in front of another picture, and both are seen simultaneously.

Sync Synchronization; the simultaneous projection of picture and sound; also, the electronic pulses of picture transmitter and receiver must be synchronized to produce a stable image on the television screen.

Tag An addition to a commercial, announcement, or musical gimmick that acts as a finale to that segment.

TCU Tight close-up; narrow angle picture. (See also: **BCU, ECU**.)

Take (1) Switching directly from one picture or camera to another picture or camera, as "take one, take two," (2) Individual filmed or taped sequences or scenes.

Talent An all-inclusive word referring to actors, announcers, musicians, or performers.

Technical director The director of all camera or video facilities from a television station.

Telephoto lens A very narrow angle lens that produces large images at extreme distance; frequently used at sporting events, etc.

Teleprompter A patented machine on which a large version of the script can be unrolled at any desired speed, operated out of camera range to prompt actors; usually mounted on the camera near the lens turret. The reader appears to look almost directly at the viewer when using a Teleprompter on live camera.

Televise To transmit a picture electronically using TV equipment.

Telop An opaque photograph or drawing projected by the telop projector.

Tight shot A picture that fills the screen with a single object of interest so that no background detail distracts from it.

Tilt A camera movement, pivoting on the horizontal axis, up or down.

Tilt-up A storyboard designation describing an upward pan of the camera. (Tilt-down is the reverse movement.)

Title crawl A device for moving a series of titles across the screen, appearing at the bottom, disappearing at the top. Often a motor-driven drum.

Title drum A large drum on which title sheets can be fastened for credit supers; the same as a crawl.

Titles Any title used on a TV program or commercial. Can be motion picture film, card, slides, etc.

Transparency A technique whereby illustrative or written material is placed on a transparent surface through which background material may be seen as the transparency is picked up by the TV camera.

Treatment An intermediate step between synopsis and script in which the complete TV story, commercial, or production is completed.

Truck A movement of a studio camera, left or right, parallel to the plane of action.

Trucking The camera moving beside a character or object that is in motion.

Truck shot A camera, mounted on a moveable dolly, is guided along a certain prescribed path marked on the studio floor. This gives an effect of moving toward, past, or away from whatever is to be filmed.

TVB Television Bureau of Advertising.

Two shot Often printed ''2-shot''; refers to a picture in which two persons are seen. (''3-shot'' includes three people.)

Viewfinder A small television set on top of the camera in which the cameraman sees the picture he is photographing.

Viewing lens The lens on a TV camera used by the cameraman to view the field of action.

Video The visual, pictorial portion of a television program, announcement, or commercial.

Videotape recording An electronic system that permits the recording of video and audio on a continuous strip of tape. It requires no laboratory processing, can be rewound and played back immediately, and can be edited immediately after recording. Film is often transferred to videotape for use in telecasting.

Voice-over (VO) In television, a commercial, film, or live sequence in which an actor's or announcer's voice is heard, but the person is not seen.

Whip shot A fast pan shot, blurring the action on the screen.

Whiz pan A camera swung very rapidly left to right or right to left, blurring the scene. Used as a dramatic device to shift from one scene to another or one object of interest to another, or for comic effects, simulating doubletake. Also known as a blur pan, swish pan, whip shot, etc.

Wide-angle lens A special lens that permits a greater view of the field, left and right.

Wide-angle shot A shot that makes it possible for the camera to cut a wide scene from a shallow depth.

Wide shot A shot that covers a large area.

Wipe An optical effect in which a line or object appears to move across the screen revealing a new picture. A wipe may stop midway and become a split-screen effect.

Wipe over Optical film or printing effect by which one scene or image moves into another geometrically.

XCU Extreme close-up; same as ECU.

Zoom The change in focal length of a special lens (Zoomar lens) that gives the effect of moving either toward or away from an object.

Zoomar An adjustable lens that can zoom from a focal length of one size to another without loss of focus or light.

Zoom lens A special lens on a motion picture and TV camera that permits slow or rapid movement either toward or away from the photographed subject. Can be used in studios or on location. Can be used to cover a great distance quickly.

Bibliography

Abrahams, Howard P. *Making TV Pay Off*. New York: Fairchild Publications, 1975.

Backman, Jules. *Advertising and Competition*. New York: New York University Press, 1967.

Baldwin, Huntley. *Creating Effective TV Commercials*. Chicago: Crain Books, 1982.

Bellaire, Arthur. *The Bellaire Guide to TV Commercial Cost Control*. Chicago: Crain Books, 1982.

Book, Albert C., and C. Dennis Schick. *Fundamentals of Copy and Layout*. Chicago: Crain Books, 1984.

Bovée, Courtland L., and William F. Arens. *Contemporary Advertising*. Homewood, Ill.: Richard D. Irwin, 1983.

Burroughs, Thomas D., and Donald N. Wood. *Television Productions: Disciplines and Techniques*. Dubuque, Iowa: Wm. C. Brown Co., 1978.

Burton, Philip W., and William Ryan. *Advertising Fundamentals*. Columbus, Ohio: Grid Publishing Co., 1980.

Busch, H. Ted, and Terry Landeck. *The Making of a Television Commercial*. New York: Macmillan Publishing Co., Inc., 1980.

Costa, Sylvia Allen. *How to Prepare a Production Budget for Film and Video Tape*. Blue Ridge Summit, Pa.: TAB Books, 1975.

Diamont, Lincoln, ed. *Anatomy of a Television Commercial*. New York: Hastings House, 1970.

Heighton, Elizabeth, and Don R. Cunningham. *Advertising in the Broadcast Media*. Belmont, Calif.: Wadsworth Publishing Co., 1980.

Hilliard, Robert L. *Writing for Television and Radio*. New York: Hastings House, 1976.

Kaatz, Ronald B. *Cable: An Advertiser's Guide to the New Electronic Media*. Chicago: Crain Books, 1982.

Mandell, Maurice I. *Advertising*. 3rd ed. Englewood Cliffs, N.J.: Prentice-Hall, 1980.

Price, Jonathan. *The Best Thing on TV, Commercials*. New York: Viking Press, 1978.

Peck, William A. *Anatomy of Local Radio-TV Copy*. Blue Ridge Summit, Pa.: TAB Books, 1976.

Robinson, Sol. *Radio Advertising*. Blue Ridge Summit, Pa.: TAB Books, 1974.

Roman, Kenneth, and Jane Maas. *How to Advertise*. New York: St. Martin's Press, 1977.

Sandage, Charles H., et al. *Advertising: Theory and Practice*. 11th ed. Homewood, Ill.: Richard D. Irwin, 1983.

Steiner, Gary. *The People Look at Television*. New York: Alfred A. Knopf, 1963.

Wainwright, Charles Anthony. *How to Create Successful TV Advertising*. New York: Hastings House, 1975.

White, Hooper. *How to Produce an Effective TV Commercial*. Chicago: Crain Books, 1981.

Willing, Si. *How to Sell Radio Advertising*. Blue Ridge Summit, Pa.: TAB Books, 1970.

Witek, John. *Response Television: Combat Advertising of the 1980s*. Chicago: Crain Books, 1981.

Wright, John S., et al. *Advertising*. 5th ed. New York: McGraw-Hill, 1982.

Wurtzel, Alan. *Television Production*. New York: McGraw-Hill, 1979.

Young, James Webb. *A Technique for Producing Ideas*. Chicago: Crain Books, 1970.

Zeigler, Sherilyn K. and Herbert H. Howard. *Broadcast Advertising*. 2nd ed. Columbus, Ohio: Grid Publishing Co., 1983.

Zettl, Herbert. *Television Production Handbook*. Belmont, Calif.: Wadsworth Publishing Co., 1977.